From Classroom to Boardroom
In support of HIT Scotland

EP, 4 Lombard Street, London EC3V 9HD
020 7933 8760
www.epmagazine.co.uk

First Published in Great Britain in 2017 by EP Business in Hospitality

© **EP Business in Hospitality** is part of Chess Executive Ltd. Every effort is made to ensure the accuracy of the information contained in this publication. Reproduction or use of this material without permission of Chess Executive Ltd is prohibited. The opinions expressed herein are not necessarily those of the editor/publisher.

ISBN: 978-0-9957033-0-8

Designed by **Newhall Publishing Ltd**
New Hall Lane, Hoylake, Wirral CH47 4BQ
0844 545 8102
www.newhallpublishing.com

Printed by **Gomer Press Limited**
Llandysul Enterprise Park, Llandysul, Ceredigion SA44 4JL
01559 362371
www.gomer.co.uk

Contents

Introduction — 9
David Cochrane and Peter Lederer CBE

My personal reflection — 11
Angela Vickers

Foreword — 13
No one can afford not to be open to learning anymore – Chris Sheppardson

Chapter 1 — 19
Developing the Hospitality Leaders of Tomorrow – Alan Wilson

Chapter 2 — 25
The Changing Role of the Hotel General Manager – Laurie Nichol

Chapter 3 — 35
The Impact of General Manager Succession Policies – Jochem-Jan Sleiffer

Chapter 4 — 43
Developing an Effective Hospitality Leadership Strategy for Generation Y – the Millennial – Angela Vickers

Chapter 5 — 51
Talent Management in the Hospitality Industry – Torsten Pinter

Chapter 6 — 59
Employer Branding and its Role Within the Hospitality Industry – Richard Ellison

Chapter 7 — 65
Attracting Hospitality Graduates – Gerhard Struger

Chapter 8 — 69
Enhancing the Attractiveness of Entry Level Hospitality Jobs – Jennifer Neil

Chapter 9 — 75
Social Media and Employee Recruitment – Marcus-Milan Arandelovic

Chapter 10 — 81
Developing an Innovative Corporate Culture – Joanne Taylor-Stagg

Chapter 11 — 87
Boutique and Lifestyle Brand Positioning – Beverly Payne

Chapter 12 — 93
The Impact of Recession on Consumer Behaviour and Implications for the Hotel Industry in the UK and Ireland – Craig Gardner

Chapter 13 — 99
Marketing Hotels to Generation Y – Alok Dixit

Chapter 14 — 103
The Impact of Social Media Marketing on Hotel Success – Thomas Healy

Chapter 15 — 109
Trends in Hotel Distribution – Yousif Al-Wagga

Chapter 16 — 115
The Impact of UGC on Restaurant Success – Edward Harvey

Chapter 17 — 121
Understanding the Potential of International Sporting Events – Stuart Smith

Chapter 18 — 127
Disintermediation of Hotel Distribution – Clinton Campbell

Chapter 19 — 133
Drowning in the Red Ocean: Hotels, Technology and the Customer – Peter Stack

Chapter 20 — 139
Service Recovery in the Hotel Industry – Jonathan Walker

Chapter 21 — 145
Hotel Loyalty and Generation Y – Simon Davis

Reference section — 150

Introduction

●

By David Cochrane, Chief Executive HIT Scotland

and Peter Lederer CBE

The industry has undergone many challenges over the lifespan of the Executive Masters programme. The great learning opportunities provided on the programme have also competed with global challenges of finance, uncertainty and disrupted travel. These challenges led to greater analysis of participants businesses and more decision making scenarios being built into the syllabus.

The learning on the programme has also equipped the sector with better strategic leadership and the outcomes from many individuals have been commercially effective. The return on investment for individual participation, plus the business benefits delivered by the programme, have been immense. Savings and systems have been implemented that have produced stunning results for the industry and many of these ideas have originated through classroom discussion and peer to peer examination of challenges that the industry faces.

The modular approach to learning that they undertook, has also been instilled across many parts of the industry. Short, sharp interventions provided the theory, coupled with expertise already within the industry globally, and the knowledge and friendships gained from the Executive Masters, will live with each and every individual for the rest of their careers. We are delighted that this learning has been kept alive through the compilation of these executive summaries, published from the three Cohorts over the last few years. They give a fascinating insight into leadership, and we wish every success, to all participants, into the future.

My personal reflection

●

By Angela Vickers

Chief Executive Officer, Apex Hotels

"Not Looking down the lens of a microscope, rather, looking up through the lens of a telescope." This sentence sums up my personal experience of the program. Looking beyond the 'tunnel vision' of day to day priorities, by expanding horizons and executing strategies rather than just creating them.

The Executive Masters in Hospitality and Tourism Leadership program was a unique and bespoke initiative created by three of the most well respected hospitality and business education providers, namely University of Strathclyde Business School, Cornell University and Ecole Hôtelière de Lausanne. This formation devised a world class syllabus that better equipped the participants to deal more expertly with the pace of change in a dynamic sector. The program was so far reaching and innovative in its approach that there was a true transformation from Management to Global Leaders, graduates emerged more confident and self-aware, adept problem solvers, better strategists and game changers.

There was a realisation that industry and academia can work collaboratively together to solve key challenges faced by hospitality leaders today. The contents of this book are evidence of that. This is true not just of industry and academia but within the industry. During the program we worked collaboratively with our main competitors, sharing experiences and providing support. The resultant global network of industry contacts and long standing friendships far out weighted the piece of paper proclaiming the Masters qualification. It was a pleasure and privilege to have the opportunity to experience the program, to meet fascinating people from my fellow students, lecturers and eminent professors to keynote industry and non-industry speakers.

I would urge anyone considering further study not to hesitate, the dedication required is definitely worth the rewards… it is a lifelong gain for a short term commitment!

No one can afford not to be open to learning

By Chris Sheppardson

Founder of EP Business in Hospitality

Chris is the founder of two companies within the Hospitality industry, a leading Executive management recruitment company called Chess Partnership founded in 1998 and EP Magazine in 2005 which produces two industry titles, has a strategic consultancy practice, supports young entrepreneurs and innovation in the Industry, hosts Think Tanks and around 65 events a year on leading issues of the day.

Chris is a great believer in both emerging talent and the opportunities and careers that the industry provides. Chris is also a Trustee of two Industry charities, a patron of the Edge Hotel School and a published author of 5 books, most notably with one on leaders and entrepreneurs in Hospitality and two on sport.

There has been so much written about the pace of change and it is remarkable but the one truth that remains is that everyone – however old or young – needs to be open to learning new ideas and skills. This is arguably the first time in history whereby the older generation are learning new skills from the younger generation but it is also true that the latter do need the skills of the former just as much. The Baby Boomers led lives based on actions. Gen Y is more strategic and global. They both need the other and all need to be open to learning and listening to new ideas and concepts. The world is changing at such pace, it is easy to miss key pieces of information.

Most business books are based on the philosophies and experiences of proven business leaders and expert observers. This is different. The value of the following text is that the works have been developed by today's emerging leaders – those that are the future leaders and working at the sharp end of the industry. There have been very few business books written by an audience of emerging leaders and it is fair to say that all those that are published, have returned to their companies after the MBA programme and created new initiatives and seen their careers develop. The following does therefore really possess genuine importance and is thought-provoking.

In a recent discussion that EP had with MBA students at a Swiss Hotel School, the students talked proudly of the way that modern comms has made the world open and transparent and that there is free information at everyone's fingertips. It is true. The modern flow of information has arguably led to increased process, analysis and transparency. The emerging leaders of today do see the world and industry through different eyes and the following does shed light on a range of issues.

The Gen Y group do believe in the environment and in changing the world and one can easily see that they will leave the world in a better place than was inherited.

A recent PWC report entitled "The Future of work. The journey to 2022." Illustrates just how much is changing and how fast. This report draws on a specially commissioned survey of 10,000 people in China, India, Germany, the UK and the US, who told how they think the workplace will evolve and how this will affect their employment prospects and future working lives. Further input comes from a survey of almost 500 HR professionals across the world.

A quick glance immediately tells you that:
- 66% see the future of work as a world full of possibility and believe they will be successful
- 53% think technological breakthroughs will transform the way people work over the next 5-10 years

They publish a chart that tells a powerful story of change over the last ten years:
2006 – The launch of twitter
2007 – The launch of the Apple iPhone
2008 – The fall of Lehman Brothers as it files for bankruptcy
2009 – The first year when the world urban population exceeds those living in rural areas.
2010 – China overtakes the USA as the world's largest manufacturer
2011 – The world's populations exceed 7 billion
2013 – The number of mobile devices and connections surpasses the number of people on the planet
2015 - Worker in Germany says the "best is yet to come" after celebrating 75 years' service with the same firm
2016 - $10 tablet computer comes on to the market

The above illustrates very clearly a world that is in continuous social and economic change. The world will invariably become more automated and the differences between businesses – whether large or small – will become less and less as each company will possess the same technology and access to the same information.

Foreword

The one real difference between companies will be the people. This leads to two points:
1. Over the last two decades there has been a relative decline in the investment made into people. However, people will be the major differential that will set businesses apart and most especially, Hospitality businesses. Yes, there will be robot and automated hotels but research suggests that nothing will beat the personal touch that great people led service can engender.
2. The chances are that the world will become increasingly intelligent and process led. There are skills to be learnt from the Baby Boomers who did often act out of instinct first and were a generation that understood human failure and weakness. They may have been a selfish generation but they were also a very generous generation as they did believe in teams and friendship.

Both the above are important as great service cultures can only be developed out of empathy and actions, not intelligence and process.

Of course, there will be those that will counter with the example of Google glasses or the way that hotels can research their guests far more thoroughly but it does not match the moment a hotelier sees a guest in pain, or in need and instinctively helps that person.

There is a story of one London General Manager – a Baby Boomer – who was in a taxi in the rain and saw one of the occasional guests walking the rain. He stopped the taxi and gave the guest a lift to their destination even though it cost him an extra £10. The return was loyalty and gratitude from the guest which gave back exponentially far more than the £10 cost.

Of course, anyone of any age could have done this. But so often we are all so busy that we would not have seen outside the cab. It is a different mindset that saw the picture and helped.

Hospitality is not just a service anymore; it is also theatre/entertainment. Research is showing that people are eating out more and more and that they want to see new ideas, original concepts and to be constantly entertained and challenged. There is a view that F&B strategies can no longer be reviewed annually but almost in quarterly cycles as the market is moving at such a pace.

Sports are becoming increasingly important. There is a convergence of sport and fitness with hospitality. There has never before been any major commercial convergence of the sports and hospitality industry in Europe and a significant gap in the market exists for a credible sports resort to cater for both professional and amateur sports participants, their families, team mates and friends.

In past eras, sport was simply a form of recreation for all but the very top athletes. Today it has become a serious business. In 2016, sport is far more than a pastime for those that embrace it and there are huge numbers today embracing sport. In 2016, the number of executives exercising four times per week has grown by 17%. In recent years, sport has become increasingly central to everyday life and also big business in its own right as major brands such as Nike and Adidas have become household names and brands. The momentum for change has been supported by a social revolution, which has seen personal fitness grow in importance with each passing. Last year the two fastest growing "exercises" were Triathlon and Pilates. The largest sports across Europe today are swimming, running and cycling and this trend will continue as personal fitness becomes more and more part of daily lifestyles.

There is an increased desire for great spa facilities and operations. Spas are an option for self-reward and indulgence and this is now becoming a primary area of focus for the guest. Good Spas can also act as a method for building links and relationships with the local community and make hotels real centres for the locality as well as the visitor.

There is a need today for the interactive whereby there is more natural action between the hotel and the guest. This can extend to include the theatre of chefs cooking, or guests cooking together and preparing their own meals or to just the natural theatre experienced within restaurants.

The welcome is vital. Research has shown that most guests are more inclined to dwell for longer, spend more and return more readily if they are welcomed warmly. One of the great frustrations with hotels is that welcomes are often poor although there is a belief that this is improving considerably.

The Market will be increasingly driven by younger demographics. Hotels need to consider how they are attracting the next generation of guests, if at all? It is important to start establishing plans for developing this audience as it is laying the ground for tomorrow. Research shows that the changes in the market are being driven by those aged between 18-35. The older generations still remain relatively loyal to core food styles but will experiment and taste new food styles. The younger generation however are very experimental, are eating out more often than any previous generation and want far broader food style options.

Considering the above, future menu development must take a variety of key influencers into consideration to ensure that both generations are engaged and catered for.

- Responsible consumption – a commitment towards sustainability and environmental programmes
- Premiumised informality in environment and style of service
- Inspirational and adventurous food styles
- Well-being and health
- Trusted value

There is no doubt that the issues of sustainability and nutrition have moved from being a peripheral strategic consideration to needing to be core/central. These considerations are here to stay and will only continue to become of increasing importance. The emerging generations will want to see companies committed to being more sustainably and environmentally friendly. There is a belief that the focus is too much on cost and not enough on revenue growth. Thankfully, the overall food standards have and continue to improve and there is greater investment in chefs and culinary. The days of the celebrity chef is on the decline but chefs are today seen as real craftsmen and clients are seeking greater investment into this area. Clients too want to see the development of hotels as Social Hubs for communication and social networking.

Some of the above may be seen as slightly extreme but there is little doubt that the consumer wants to be excited by original ideas, theatre, emotion and experience that can display something very special. This does open up a plethora of opportunity. One may question but the reality is that the concept of high speed delivery of food to homes and offices will become increasingly successful. There are already new online concepts being developed which will grow exponentially at speed as they can serve a substantial audience with no High Street presence and take the food directly to the consumer rather than have/own a lease and wait for the consumer to arrive. Again isn't this another natural area of innovation for Food Service companies?

The consumer is less engaged by brands and more engaged with a passion for food and for diet. It is all about exceptional food and service, theatre and emotion, experience and stories. This could mark an exciting opportunity for those within the hospitality industry that can grasp the concept and create great solutions.

Whatever happens, the truth is still that the world is changing at pace and that to adapt and excel we all need to be open and learn – often from some of the best teachers in our industry – the emerging talent and leaders.

Developing the Hospitality Leaders of Tomorrow

●

By Professor Alan Wilson

University of Strathclyde Business School

Alan Wilson was the Academic Director for the Masters in Hospitality Leadership programme. He is Professor of Services Marketing at Strathclyde University Business School, Scotland and a Visiting Professor at École hôtelière de Lausanne, Switzerland.

Alan has written numerous articles and advised many public and private organisations on marketing, branding, service delivery and customer experience management.

He is co-author of the European edition of Services Marketing: Integrating Customer Focus Across the Firm, now in it's third edition.

The hospitality industry has experienced significant change over the last 15 years. There has been the growth in online travel agents, online review sites such as TripAdvisor, mergers of major hotel chains, the launch of Airbnb, the growth of boutique and lifestyle brands, an increase in global travel, changes in operational and customer facing technology as well as differences in the ways that consumers want to engage with and relate to organisations and brands. Within this context, the hospitality leaders of today and tomorrow need to develop, grow and adapt. They need to think beyond the traditional ways of doing things, be open to new ideas and have the opportunity to stand-back from the day to day operations and see the bigger picture. This can sometimes be difficult for a General Manager or Area General Manager in an industry where the product is produced and delivered in real time with the customer present. Managing the day to day often

becomes more critical than planning for the long term. As a result, some hotel chains have sought leaders from outside the hospitality sector employing senior managers from FMCG companies, airlines and accountancy firms rather than developing their own leadership talent. There is nothing wrong with this approach on a limited scale as it brings in new ideas and management approaches, however, there is also a need for leaders who know the industry and understand the true meaning of hospitality.

The Executive MSc in Hospitality Leadership was launched in 2012 to address this need and enhance the leadership capacity of the hospitality industry. An industry steering group worked in collaboration with the University of Strathclyde Business School, Scotland and supported by Cornell University, USA and École hôtelière de Lausanne, Switzerland with funding from the Scottish Funding Council to develop the programme aimed at training the hospitality leaders of tomorrow. Three cohorts of senior managers attended the two-year programme on a part time basis and each participant has contributed a chapter of this book based on their final dissertations. The overall programme aimed to provide professional progression opportunities for participants and this has been reflected in 66% of the participants being promoted or having moved to more senior positions in other organisations during and after completion of the programme.

However, recruitment of participants has been an on-going challenge throughout the whole programme. Major international marketing and sales efforts have been made by the University and the International Leadership School in collaboration with the Hospitality Industry Trust Scotland. These have involved a wide range of events, advertising, media coverage, social media activity and partial scholarships. This still resulted in relatively small cohort numbers. As a result, the programme has now ended and this book is part of the legacy of this whole initiative.

So why did the initiative grind to a halt. It wasn't that GMs didn't want to do the programme, it was generally because they could not get the support or funding from their employers to attend. This may be partially due the fact that the hospitality industry does not have a track record of making significant investments in the professional development of their general managers. Maybe some hospitality organisations are not truly concerned about developing leaders, they want effective managers as leadership skills come from experience on the job and there is no need to expose managers to new ideas and thinking. There may also be confusion as to who should pay for GM development. Should it be the hotel owners or the hotel brands?

Whatever the reason, it is a fact that the hospitality industry will need strong leaders as the route ahead for hotels will continue to see significant change in the years to come.

So What Makes a Leader in Hospitality?

Testa and Sipe (2012) state that leaders in hospitality need to be business-savvy (setting objectives; business planning; understanding and attracting the correct target market; managing revenue and costs), people-savvy (developing teams; influencing corporate culture; creating support networks using effective communication and interpersonal skills) and self-savvy (being self-aware; professional; self developing; accountable and adaptable). All managers will already be well-developed in some of these areas and less competent in others. Traditional leadership training is about plugging the gaps, there are separate training programmes on skill building areas such as communication skills, team building skills, revenue management etc. However, in the fast changing world in which we operate, leaders need to develop a higher level of more holistic skills to be effective. The hospitality industry require leaders who are:

Global Watchers

Leaders need to be able to consider and interpret social, cultural, political, environmental, geographic, and economic issues and their likely impact on their organisation and the hospitality industry in general. What are the implications of Brexit, currency fluctuations, migration, technology, the sharing economy? Where are the future growth markets? Who and what are the competition? To be proactive and successful, scenario planning becomes critical. In an article in Harvard Business Review, Wack wrote:

"Scenarios deal with two worlds; the world of facts and the world of perceptions. They explore for facts but they aim at perceptions inside the heads of decision-makers. Their purpose is to gather and transform information of strategic significance into fresh perceptions."

Scenario planning is not about predicting the future, it is about bringing together different perspectives to determine a range of distinct futures. It is a methodological approach for strategy development in organisations acting in a highly dynamic environment taking complex and often risky decisions. It can provide rigour as well as opportunities to draw upon the creativity of those involved, resulting in new views and interpretations on important external developments. The leadership challenge is to consider how to deal with each of the scenarios identified across the whole of the organisation whether in relation to employment, marketing, investment or operations.

Strategic Opportunists

The internet has led to many disruptive innovations that create new market niches and value networks which can displace established brands, products and alliances. In the hospitality sector, online travel agents, Airbnb, and TripAdvisor are just some of these disruptive innovations. It is therefore important that leaders seek out strategic opportunities ahead of their competitors and other innovators. This means an obsession with customers and the customer experience. It requires leaders to observe consumers and their behaviour in domestic and foreign markets. What are they doing? How are their tastes changing? What expectations do they have? Are millennials different? What do the growing band of elderly want to do with their money and leisure time? There is a need to gauge the pulse of modern culture.

It is combining this keen interest in customers with a shrewd sense of timing to advance these opportunities for the betterment of the company in the longer term. It may also involve searching for internal strategic opportunities to improve the product offering, service delivery or operations to address future customer expectations. This requires thinking time and the ability to stand back from the day to day operations to identify and address the opportunities. In-boxes full of emails, smartphone messages, congested social media feeds and the noise of modern life can distract leaders from looking at future opportunities. However, it is unlikely that an organisation can simply perpetuate a system where things are done in the same way that they have always been done. There are always methods of doing things differently and only by getting out of the office or hotel can a leader know what is hot or not.

Orchestral Conductors

"The craft of conducting a classical orchestra may be described as an art of persuasion by which musicians, audiences, and communities come to share a deep connection with the orchestra and its repertoire. Passion, intellect, insight, musical talent, and charisma all come into play. A conductor's authority flows from the respect he or she commands, the power of his or her musical vision, and the skill and facility by which musical ideas are communicated through physical movement as well as verbal instructions." (League of American Orchestras)

As hospitality structures become more complicated, it is critical that leaders can act as a form of orchestral conductor to ensure that all the functions are working together for a common goal. With the growth in the centralisation of reservations, centralisation of revenue management operations, centralisation of human resource functions and outsourced food and beverage operations, the role of the leader has become more complex. There may be cross-functional project teams focusing on different initiatives across the organisation with team members reporting to different functional heads. Similar to an orchestra where you may have the wind section, the string section, the brass section and the percussion section, all having their own lead and potentially rehearsing separately, there is a need for a conductor to pull it all together and deliver the perfect performance. This requires effective coordination and coaching as well as networking through strategic alliances. These strategic alliances in orchestras may be external choirs and venues but in hospitality, they may be with outsourced services, event planners and online travel agents. This requires a broad understanding of all these functions as well as the persuasive capabilities to motivate individuals without trying to dictate behaviour. The aim should be to develop an internal environment that enhances employee and supplier/sub-contractor effectiveness.

Cultural Diplomats

There is a growing need for leaders to be able to understand and manage multinational teams and individuals from various ethnic backgrounds. This is of importance to operators working in a single country just as much as it is for the multinational hotel brands. It requires an understanding of the different values and perceptions that different groups may hold. This may impact on their attitude to work, their attitude to empowerment or authority and how they relate to different customer groups. Cultural differences can create significant obstacles to effective teamwork and the leaders can often cause more problems by intervening. The leaders of tomorrow need to be empathetic and diplomatic in leading these different cultural groups. They need to understand how to guide their management teams to establish cohesive work groups and manage their employees' relationships with customers of different nationalities, races and genders.

Charismatic Community Builders

Leaders need to be respected. They don't necessarily need to be liked but they need to be respected and viewed as effective role models as well as being a trusted spokesperson for the organisation. Respect comes from being seen as one who has performed to reach the top rather than simply being one who simply persevered and hung around long enough to achieve that position. They also need to be seen as trusting their staff through empowering them whilst at the same time being viewed as the trusted leader who will address their employees' concerns as well as support and stand by them. To be effective, the leader's words and actions must be congruent and consistent. Similar to a successful brand, leaders need to be seen as authentic where their actions and persona represent their true nature or beliefs.

In Conclusion

Some authors talk about the need for transformational leadership but all leadership needs to be transformational to a greater or lesser degree otherwise it is simply a management and administrative function. It is about having a broad, holistic perspective of the current and future success of the organisation rather than simply managing the daily operational needs of the organisation. A pro-active rather than reactive approach to guiding the organisation is needed for the current and future challenges of the hospitality industry.

To achieve this, there is not a standard leadership toolkit that can be taught to managers, it is about exposing them to different people, viewpoints, situations and experiences combined with providing an opportunity for self-reflection and thinking time. That is what the Executive Masters in Hospitality Leadership was designed to do and the following quotes suggest that the programme went some way towards achieving that:

"An important opportunity for me has been the chance to 'open my eyes' to the world outside Hilton. I needed this to move from a purely operational job to my current strategic level role." *Jochem Jan Sleiffer, Area Vice President Northern and Central Europe, Hilton Worldwide*

"Even though you think you know the hospitality industry from the inside out, the programme has given new insights, broadened my approach and lifted my thinking to a next strategic level yet not losing sight of the operational framework." *Marcus-Milan Arandelovic, Area General Manager, Benelux, Hilton Worldwide*

"In comparison with more general business or MBA programmes, the Executive Masters in Hospitality Leadership is focused on issues pertinent to the sector whilst also drawing on best practice from other industries." *Angela Vickers, Chief Executive Officer, Apex Hotels*

"The programme gave me a unique opportunity to learn in the 3 most pre-eminent hospitality and business schools in the world. The education was as valuable in the classroom as it was informally speaking with fellow students. The subjects covered everything a hotelier should know but more importantly over the 2 years I have changed the way I think. I believe I am better equipped to handle the ever changing demands because of the programme." *Joanne Taylor-Stagg, General Manager, London and Regional Properties*

"The course offered invaluable networking and learning for leaders of the future. It encouraged new ways of thinking and brought a new dimension to hospitality leadership." *Laurie Nicol, Chief Operating Officer, De Vere*

The following chapters set out an abbreviated version of the dissertations undertaken by the programme participants at the end of their studies. They address topics that had a direct impact on their leadership roles at the time and have a relevance for the hospitality industry as a whole.

The Changing Role of the Hotel General Manager

By Laurie Nicol

Chief Operating Officer, De Vere

Laurie Nicol started her career in hospitality in 1989 working at the QMH hotel in Glasgow as a Banqueting Operations Manager until 1995. Thereafter she opened the Edinburgh International Conference Centre as Operations Manager and moved on to various regional sales and business development positions across Scotland and Northern England within Stakis Hotels (acquired by Hilton in 1999) where her career spanned 13 years.

In 2010, Laurie was appointed as General Manager of the Central Hotel in Glasgow where she led the £20 Million refurbishment bringing the 'Grand Dame' back to life and was delighted when the team won Scottish Hotel of the Year in 2012.

Currently employed by Principal Hayley (recently acquired by the Starwood Capital Group) Laurie spent 2 years as Regional Operations Director developing strategy for their 5 hotels in Scotland.

In October 2016 Laurie was appointed COO of De Vere and is responsible for repositioning and aligning the De Vere, Principal Hayley and Four Pillars in to one group of country house and conference led properties.

The role of hotel General Manager covers a wide variety of functions and does not have a traditional career progression path. There are many ways that GMs have made their way into their position. It was therefore of interest to investigate the most common route now compared to ten or fifteen years ago and if this has changed. If the route to the role varies so much, how can individuals bring the correct skill set to it if they all have very

different career routes that may or may not encompass experience from one or more hotel department?

In medicine for example there is a clear career path and undergraduates will know exactly what they need to do to reach the level of Consultant. They will complete their degree at University, a two-year foundation programme within a hospital and then undertake specialist training in their chosen field. In hospitality management there is no such defined career path.

Routes to General Manager
Previous Research

Traditionally, Poulston and Kim (2010) suggest that hospitality career progression can more generally be viewed as "coming up through the ranks" with employees moving from supervisory to junior or mid management before securing a more senior position such as GM.

Watson (2008) suggested that it is one of the strange characteristics of the hospitality industry that food and beverage knowledge is regarded so highly when recruiting for GM positions. Ladkin (2002) identified that only a small percentage of candidates come from human resources, sales and marketing or finance, which are the more strategic areas of the business with which GMs are more involved with on a daily basis. Garavan et al. (2006) argued that GMs should possess various areas of expertise including language and communication, people management, entrepreneurial skills as well as being a competent manager within the operation. Watson (2008) further develops this concluding that leadership, corporate and strategic skills are now shown to be at the forefront in the career progression of young GMs.

Current Study Findings

It has been identified in past studies that there is no clear career path to become a GM. Today, some GMs have a food and beverage back ground, but four other departments feature highly as areas where GMs had gained the most experience. These are finance, revenue management, sales and front office with revenue management being the second most popular route.

There are some hotel departments that were identified as having no career path to GM, these being maintenance and human resources. It could be assumed that these departments are specialist and are unlikely to have working knowledge of any department other than their own. One company interviewed had a GM who had progressed from the kitchen and one had a GM with a housekeeping background. It can be concluded that these career paths are unusual and individuals would have to be exceptional to move from these areas of expertise into the role of GM.

All of the hotel groups interviewed cited that revenue management experience was now a necessary requirement in the role of GM. While most respondents mentioned food and beverage experience as a necessity, not all did which illustrates that the hotel business is changing and the importance of food and beverage is being overtaken by revenue management.

In terms of developing internal candidates, many hotel companies had stopped their management development programmes in the last 5 years due to cost constraints.

Of those that did have internal programmes for deputy GMs or operations managers to work their way towards GM level within their company, the contents of the programmes included 'off the job' training in areas such as:

- Sales skills
- Revenue management
- Human resources management
- Internal IT systems
- Financial management
- Customer loyalty
- Social media particularly Trip Advisor
- Online travel agencies
- Marketing
- Personal presentation
- Budgeting process
- Statutory compliance

Interestingly, not one of the programmes covers the food and beverage area of the business as it may be assumed that anyone at this level would have basic knowledge in this area or that the importance of F&B is diminishing and commercial aspects have become more important.

The requirement for a degree before entering the management programme varied from organisation to organisation. The smaller hotel chains do not require candidates to be in possession of one whilst the larger chains do. Interestingly one chain that did seek graduates at present stated that they are finding it harder to get suitable candidates and are considering removing the degree stipulation. When representatives of the industry were asked directly if the most successful GMs were graduates or had 'worked their way up' it became clear that there was no preference either way. It can be concluded that there is scope for promotion to the role of GM without a University qualification and that most hotel companies from the sample group supported ongoing learning and development of their people.

Skill set of a GM
Previous Research

The literature on the skill set of General Managers has been examined over the last 25 years and it can be concluded that like the role itself, the skill set required has changed. Going back to the original research conducted by Worsfold (1989) the following characteristics were identified as essential for the role of GM: people skills, resilience, motivation, personality and intelligence. Although this research is dated, these are still important skills which the GM must have in order to perform their role. Chung-Herra, Enz and Lankau (2003) identified eight characteristics which are essential for successful GMs, these are listed in order of importance; self-management, strategic positioning, implementation (including planning and delegation) critical thinking, communication, interpersonal skills, leadership and industry knowledge. Studies into the skills of GMs have called for managers to be trained in presentation skills, communication, interpersonal skills, languages, critical thinking and accountancy (Ladkin, 2000 and Harkison et al 2011). Jauhari (2006) further developed this claiming that the skills required of a GM have changed with the job itself and that GMs now need to be more aware of global exposure, profitability and market trends as well as having an understanding of financial awareness and being innovative while still being committed to the goals of the organisation. Wadongo (2011) suggested that along with technical abilities, GMs must have motivation and ability to gain support from their peers as well as soft skills such as empathy, delegating effectively, creative thinking, conflict management, managing change and commitment.

Current Study Findings

At interview all respondents were asked what skills and attributes they considered essential for a GM within their company and if there were any specific skills that their company looked for that other companies did not. The information received on this subject was extremely detailed therefore it is included in a table below:

Company	Skills Required/Comments	Company Specific Skills/Comments
Hotel Group A	Good judgement Entrepreneurial Flair Operational Strength Need to be able to relate to departmental managers Good motivator HR Management Good financial acumen Commercially aware Marketing Sales Relationship management Deliver on standards Disciplined Structured Leadership skills Emotional intelligence Resilience Good communicator Target and goal driven	Passion Motivation to drive a business forward Recover from challenges or knocks Ask for support from head office as necessary Self-motivators No manuals to follow such as those found find in big international brand hotels Particular focus on sales and revenue Creativity
Hotel Group B	People management Ability to multi-task Commercially aware Analytical Self-motivated	International brand background Able to follow instructions from the 'centre' i.e. head office Commerciality

Hotel Group C	Leadership skills Good communicator Good team engagement Commercially aware Operational understanding Market knowledge Manage owner relationships	Leadership skills Experience of 'owner relationships'
Hotel Group D	Team spirit Creative thinking Good motivator Good communicator Technically competent	Good cultural fit Not a big group background
Hotel Group E	Good leadership Figurehead of the business Represent core values of the company Good influencer Good motivator Strong communication skills Sales knowledge Revenue skills Financial acumen Analytical, able to get a deal over the line Drive and determination Creative thinking	Creativity Act on own initiative No hierarchy like company like Hilton might have Must take ownership and responsibility for their business This type of manager is hard to find Hilton and Marriott give manuals, we do not Live our core values of positive, willing, consistent and genuine, friendly
Hotel Group F	Manage and understand people IT knowledge Financial acumen Awareness of Health and Safety	People skills Understand true hospitality Finance and IT both critical
Hotel Group G	Strategic Good operational skills Sales knowledge Revenue ability Human resources knowledge Engineering awareness Ability to multi-skill	Mobility Strategic Willingness to move discipline within the organisation
Hotel Group H	Good communication skills Get the best from people Strong team management Manage expectations of shareholders Drive Ability to change the direction of a business	A true hotelier as we are run by hoteliers and not banks Understand the importance of food quality and provenance Must think for themselves

Hotel Group I	Commercial awareness Ability to grow profit Sales skills Cost management Engage with team at all levels to get the best from them Excellent customer service	Nothing more specific.
Hotel Group J	Critical thinking and problem solving skills Financial acumen Sales, marketing and revenue skills Inspirational leadership Develops talent Strong communicator	Independent thinker Operations experience Strong financial acumen Influencer of change
Hotel Recruitment Agency	Knowledge of KPI's Know the competition Good education Previous experience Commercial skills Accounting knowledge Cost management Capital expenditure experience	It was highlighted by this respondent that different types of companies will have different requirements. The respondent indicated that company 'types' could be defined as 'full service' or 'budget'.

The table above demonstrates a cross section of opinion from various hotel chains in the UK and whilst the list is not exhaustive it could be used as a strong source of skill set requirements of a GM in the industry today. Worth noting from these responses is the emergence of two different types of GM. They could be defined as either a 'full service GM' or a 'limited service GM'. A full service GM would be operating many revenue streams i.e. restaurant, bar, spa, bedrooms and conference rooms whilst a limited service GM may only have responsibility for a small number of bedrooms and breakfast service. It should be noted that whilst the title of the role is the same the responsibilities are very different.

Successful GMs were perceived at better demonstrating:

- Relationship management skills
- Leading and motivating people skills
- A hunger to succeed
- Being brave when making decisions
- Entrepreneurial abilities
- Creativity
- An ability not to procrastinate
- An ability to grab opportunities when you can
- A sense of ownership for everything that they do
- Determination

- Drive and resilience
- An ability to surround themselves with driven people
- Commercially minded
- An understanding of their customer and their needs
- An ability to adapt their style to get the most out of people
- A focus on the goals of your company

It became clear that the role of the GM has seen substantial changes in the last decade. When the respondents were asked how much they thought the role of GM had changed, they used words such as significantly, dramatically, enormously, substantially and hugely. The main areas identified by the respondents that have created change in the role of GM are revenue management, centralisation of some functions, less time to be 'Mein Host', legislation and technology.

There is now an urgency to manage bedroom performance as results can be viewed by head office on a daily basis and GMs will be expected to react quickly if they are not performing to their revenue forecast. Commerciality in the business is important across all areas and not just bedrooms. GMs are expected to carefully monitor profitability in all areas and each area of the business now has an independent Profit and Loss account to record its performance. The result is that the GM is constantly monitoring pricing and costs to ensure the best profit conversion.

Many hotel groups have moved towards centralisation of some functions which would previously have been based on property. The respondents noted that in most cases revenue management, marketing and some accounting functions were managed or partly managed through clustering, the cluster office having responsibility for more than one hotel. The reason why there has been an emergence of clustering is that it is difficult to find enough specialists with expertise in that area and also patterns and synergies can be more easily identified if data for more than one hotel is being considered. There are also cost saving benefits to clustering as it is likely that an office concentrating on only one task is less likely to be distracted by other hotel activities. Accordingly, the GM will now be expected to remotely manage members of their team who are based in another location in a 'cluster' office. The GMs need to ensure that they get their fair share of this shared resource; it has been identified as a skill by the respondents to ensure that this happens.

It is believed that in a clustering situation it is possible that a GM will not have the same detailed knowledge of some areas of the business that less centralised hotel GMs may have. If revenue, finance, sales and potentially human resources are managed off property, it is possible that the GM will be less exposed to day to day knowledge of these areas. If the GM was to then move to another company who did not have centralised functions, it may be that their ability to manage these areas would be diminished. These concerns were echoed by four of the respondents who agreed that this could be a potential problem.

'Mein Host' is a commonly used term in the hotel industry. It refers to the GM as being the face of the business or as referred to in the literature, the 'Victorian greeter'. In the past the GM would be expected to be the figurehead of the business and would meet clients on arrival, particularly VIP's or organisers of large events. It has been observed by some that this is no longer possible as the GM is more likely to focus on office-based tasks due to the increasing complexities of the business. Whilst that does appear to be the case, there are concerns that to be an effective GM it is important to review customer experiences on a daily basis. It is believed that the GM must make an effort to be 'on the floor' regularly to keep in touch with their business and assess where standards need to be reviewed or amended.

In terms of legislation, GMs have more legal requirements to consider than ever before. These are in the areas of human resources and health and safety. This is driven by the emergence of the 'claim culture' and the need for companies not to be exposed to the threat of legal action. Therefore the GM needs to pay more attention to these areas to ensure compliance. Whilst the human resources manager and maintenance manager are likely to take ownership of these areas, it can also take a substantial amount of the GMs time due to the potential risks of non-compliance.

Technology has had a dramatic impact of the role of the GM with daily performance information being delivered online, comments and reviews appearing on social media sites and review sites such as TripAdvisor, online travel agents and being contactable 24 hours a day by mobile phone or email. The technological revolution has meant that GMs have many daily considerations that they would not have had a decade ago.

The Age & Gender of GMs
Previous Research

Mooney and Ryan (2009) suggest hospitality as an industry faces a worldwide shortage of adequately trained hospitality staff and as a result it is important to identify whether age or gender have an impact in recruiting and retaining successful GMs. Mooney and Ryan (2009) suggest that the glass ceiling metaphor can be applied to hospitality and is an impenetrable barrier which prevents women from moving through the managerial hierarchy. For female managers, the lines between work and social life become blurred which can be difficult for women to manage with the demands of managing a household. (Mooney & Ryan, 2009)

Current Study Findings

The table below illustrates the average age of a GM and also the percentage of female GMs employed by each hotel chain taking part in the research:

Company	Approximate age of GMs	Approximate % of Female GMs
Hotel Group A	42	30%
Hotel Group B	43	10%
Hotel Group C	43	10%
Hotel Group D	41	0%
Hotel Group E	34	25%
Hotel Group F	35	15%
Hotel Group G	44	25%
Hotel Group H	40	35%
Hotel Group I	40	20%
Hotel Group J	45	0%

The research indicates that the average age of a GM is approximately 40. The respondent from the recruitment agency indicated that as a guideline the age of GMs could be summarised by hotel types. Budget brand GMs (e.g. Premier Inn, Travel Lodge) would be in their 20's, middle brand GMs (e.g. Marriott, Hilton) would be 30-40 and that resort GMs (e.g. Gleneagles, Celtic Manor) would be 40-50. He also noted that 10-15% of recent GM placements that they handled had been female which compared with less than 5%, ten years ago.

In the past males dominated in the GM role because historically the route to GM was through food and beverage but this was now shifting towards a preference for revenue knowledge. With the emerging importance of sales and revenue knowledge and the fact that there are far more females working in these areas of the business, it is likely that there will be more female GMs in the future. Also female GMs are thought more likely to display greater skills in empathy, communication, attention to detail and compassion.

The Future

Evidence exists from this research that there is not a shortage of GMs in the hospitality industry; however, all respondents agree that there is a shortage of "good" GMs. It is concluded that the reason for this shortage is that the role has changed at pace and the training has not developed at the same rate.

It is therefore believed to be an excellent time for aspiring managers to enter the industry as there are many opportunities for candidates to develop and follow a successful career path. One of the interesting areas of this research has been the changes in the age and gender of potential candidates for the role of GM. This research concludes that this is less of a barrier than previously anticipated with GMs being identified as young as 26 years old. It is also argued that the glass ceiling is no longer preventing women from gaining promotion within the hospitality industry with some of the respondents in the research illustrating their preference for female GMs due to the different skills that they can offer. On that note, it is suggested that a better work life balance may be more likely in the future for GMs as the role becomes more office based. The GM can no longer be "Mein Host" as they are now involved in the more strategic business elements of the business rather than spending time in the operations.

Finally, it could be argued that GMs in some instances may be less skilled in specialist areas due to the centralisation of many hotel functions. The centralisation or clustering of departments such as human resources, finance or sales takes the expertise of these departments off-site leading to a change in the skills required to perform the role of GM as they now have to manage some aspects of their business remotely. This will impact the role of GMs over the next decade as many hotel companies move to more clustered functions and should be of great interest to watch this development.

The Impact of General Manager Succession Policies

●

By Jochem-Jan Sleiffer

Area Vice President, Northern and Central Europe Hilton Worldwide

Jochem-Jan Sleiffer is responsible for Hilton's portfolio of hotels in Northern, Central & Eastern Europe, as part of Hilton's wider EMEA region and sits on the EMEA Executive Committee.

Originally graduating from the Netherlands, he obtained a bachelor's degree in Facilities Management in Deventer, the Netherlands (1990) and an EMBA degree in Hospitality and Tourism Leadership from the University of Strathclyde, Glasgow, UK (2014).

Having joined Hilton as Chief Steward at Hilton Amsterdam in 1990, he has held a number of roles across Europe over the past 26 years, including in Belgium, UK, France and Greece - where he managed the successful renovation and re-opening of the 507-room Hilton Athens. He was General Manager of Hilton London Olympia, Hilton Brussels, Area General Manager of Hilton Paddington and Hilton London Euston as well as Country General Manager for France, overseeing seven hotels.

In January 2013, Jochem-Jan was promoted to Area Vice President for Northern and Central Europe, expanding his role to include responsibility for all full-service hotels in Russia, CIS and Eastern Europe in July 2015.

In larger hotel chains the General Manager typically changes every 3-5 years. It is assumed that after such a period the General Manager is less focussed and cannot see the deficiencies or opportunities as clearly as when he/she started in the job. Current succession practices within large international hotel chains do not sufficiently take

into consideration the impact the change of General Manager can have, if any, on the organizational culture of the hotel. This raises the question: 'should management take into consideration the impact that the change of General Managers can have on the organizational culture of a hotel when it is decided to move them from one hotel to another?'

Previous Research

Several studies have analysed the impact of the succession process and planning on an organisation. Brady and Helmich (1984) concluded that succession is a traumatic event for any organization. It affects not only the members of the organization but the firm's economic and political climate as well. The departure of a General Manager creates a void which needs to be filled as soon as possible to avoid a crisis, and to guarantee a smooth transfer of leadership. The process and timing of a leadership change will be different for each company but most stages will be similar.

In order to better understand the process of leadership change, Redlich (1977) and Greenblatt (1978) defined the most notable stages within the transition period from 'initial appointment and inauguration, a honeymoon period, an adjustment and transition period, and what was termed a "new equilibrium".'

When analysing the stages above, one should not underestimate the importance of the initial appointment and inauguration. If not handled professionally, the successor might lose credibility or worse, will be delayed implementing their strategy. Dyck et al., (2002) describe the importance of successful executive succession by referring to a successful 4x100 metre relay race where a) Sequence, b) Timing, c) Baton-passing technique and d) Communication are aligned.

　　a.　Sequence: businesses need leaders with different skills in different stages of their economic and organizational life-cycle as 'the greater the similarity between the skill sets and managerial styles of the incumbent and the successor, the less likely it is that superior organizational performance will result.' (Dyck, Mauws, Starke, & Mischke, 2002, p. 159)

　　b.　Timing: suggestion is made that a speedy succession takes place in order not to lose momentum. The responsibility and authority from the incumbent has to be passed swiftly to the successor for him/her to be able to fulfil his job role.

　　c.　Baton-passing technique: due to the fact that the incumbent and the successor have different skills, managerial styles and experiences, the 'hand-over' process is sometimes inconsistent. If one does not want to 'let-go' and the new leader 'takes over' frictions could occur. Dyck et al., (2002) found in their study that title, power, control, and responsibility did not always transfer simultaneously.

　　d.　Communication: 'If the relationship between the incumbent and the successor is characterized by lack of trust, poor communication, conflict over strategy and process, or lack of a shared vision for the organization, succession is likely to be problematic.' (Dyck, Mauws, Starke, & Mischke, 2002, p. 149)

In hotels, on average, the General Manager changes every 3-5 years. There are of course exceptions where changes happen after a year or after significantly longer periods. It is suggested that frequent successions are disruptive to organizations and, therefore, result in lower firm performance (Kesner & Sebora, 1994, p. 331). Other research concludes that succession rates are higher in companies where results are already poor and so it becomes a vicious circle.

'There are at least three theories about the relationship of managerial succession to organizational performance. One theory claims that succession improves performance, one asserts that succession disrupts performance and the third maintains that succession has no effect on performance' (Allen, Panian, & Lotz, 1979, p. 167). The disruption following a manager change refers to the 'altered accepted and expected patterns of organizational behaviour, causing a deterioration in morale and productivity.' (Fizel & D'Itri, 1997) Also Hill (2005) found that 'changing managers does not affect the following year's performance, as long as the replacement manager comes from within the hierarchical structure. By contrast, if the manager is hired externally, performance during the following year is likely to drop…' (Hill, 2005). A replacement manager from within may take longer to make changes as they need more time to influence the right people and will be more careful when changing established rules and procedures.

Brad and Helmich (1984) 'suggested that the impact of succession on subsequent organizational effectiveness was contingent on a number of factors such as: (1) how effectiveness was operationalised; (2) the size, age and growth of the organization; (3) the involvement of its board; (4) the characteristics of the successor; and (5) the type of change mandated.' (Kesner & Sebora, 1994, p. 344) The characteristics of the successor, including the management style as well as the previous experience he/she has acquired, will define the change a new leader can bring. Kelly (1980) 'found that successors often worked on organizational infrastructure before tackling strategy.' (Kesner & Sebora, 1994, p. 357)

First impressions are important and this certainly applies to the arrival of a new leader. Much will depend on the situation in which the business finds itself but the arrival of a new leader will force a reaction from the people working within the organization. The first reaction to the new leader is described by Greenblatt (1983) as 'falling between the extremes of two myths. Some successors are viewed as saviours for their firm (the Messiah Myth) and in other cases, the high regard for the previous manager makes it impossible for successors to measure up (the Rebecca Myth).' (Kesner & Sebora, 1994)

Much of the change needed might also depend on the leadership style of the previous General Manager. Guest (1962) referring to P. Blau suggests that 'the person who comes in after an indulgent leader has a very difficult time trying to establish bureaucratic procedures, while the person who comes in after a disciplinarian leader can maintain bureaucratic disciplines and still not appear as disciplinarian. He can be perceived as a "good guy" because he can relax a few authoritarian measures the former administrator had instituted.'

Miller (1993) concluded his study with 'the most striking finding is that succession is associated with change, regardless of direction, in a wide variety of organizational dimensions including power dispersion, information processing, and competitive aggressiveness.

Current Research

These findings are based on depth interviews with members of the senior management team in a number of hotels and reveal a number of common themes grouped into the following categories:

Categories	Key words
Organisational standstill	Freeze period, back to zero
Change	Uncertainty, career stand still, image & reputation, self-critical, empowerment
Communication	Influence, respect, trust

Organisational standstill

Most of the respondents referred to the organisational standstill period which is created when the incumbent GM has announced his or her departure and the successor has not arrived yet. This is a period whereby respondents feel that projects are no longer pushed, nothing new is started and big decisions are pushed to the new 'soon to arrive' GM. The senior management team below the GM feel it is their responsibility to keep the business running at its best during this 'freeze' period. However, rumours on potential successors are numerous and keep many staff busy during their workday searching on Linkedin and other social media to check on the names that were rumoured as potential successors. Although the emphasis tended to be focussed on the daily activities, significant amounts of time are spent trying to understand the reputation and image of the new GM to assess their chances of being in a favourable position once he arrived.

Once the new GM has arrived, it takes time for the successor to understand the business, local culture and local market. This period was described by some as 'going back to zero' as everything was questioned and put up for discussion. Although the organizational culture and values of the hotel chain may be the same worldwide, the local culture is something that the new GM needs to get used to.

Change

This category needs to be split into several subcategories to fully understand the impact of changing the leader. This study revealed that the impact of change is felt at different times; (a) at announcement of the GM departure, (b) during the 'freeze' period and (c) the months after the new GM had started. All three periods had a different impact on the organisation and on the staff in relation to change. Some staff feel significantly lost once the current GM had announced his/her departure as the security and habits of having the established manager disappear. Some feel that their personal feelings of insecurity and uncertainty could and should not be transferred to the staff working for them and did their best to run the department as normal.

Several senior staff feel that the change of leadership made them scared and anxious and they expressed themselves as follows; 'need to prove yourself again', 'will they value my knowledge?', 'will they support my career?' For the hotel team members: 'there is a different view. I think for the team it is like a black hole. Let's say 90% of the team members do not know who this person is. What they are going to be like? What they are going to do? Will there be any changes?'

With the arrival of the new GM first impressions are important. If these first impressions are good, team leaders feel more comfortable with the change of leadership. They also express their feelings to their team in order to create confidence and remove any anxiety that may exist. New GMs adopt different ways to start in their new job and those that make changes within the first weeks of their tenure to meetings, reports etc. were seen as being more disruptive to the organisation and more likely to cause anxiety. Better GMs were those who take some time to understand the hotel and then make changes.'

This period is a time during which senior staff are more self-critical, in other words, what is the value that I bring to the company? Is the strategy still the correct one? Etc. This leads to additional work but is generally recognised as something that is needed at times to ensure the focus can be maintained. This also allows the senior staff to answer any questions from the incoming GM as a lot of information is needed during the first weeks after their arrival. So, one can say that this 'preparation of information' is self-protection against any possible criticism from the new GM and an attempt to make a good impression.

One respondent commented, 'When the new GM arrives, of course he is questioning everything. And you have to give him the insight and your knowledge and your expertise. To bring him to a level of knowledge that the former GM had. At first I perceive this negatively but then I realize it's also good for myself to review, to talk it through again, to realize things might need to be changed or should be questioned also.'

One respondent commented on GMs who want to copy and paste everything which has worked well in their previous hotel. This gives the people in the organisation the feeling that all they had done previously is not valued anymore and leads to general demotivation. It often takes up to a year until a new status quo is achieved.

Communication

All respondents commented on the communication change and its influence on the organizational culture of the hotel. Out of all of the interviews this was the most common theme. This ranges from a GM who keeps communication close to themselves and the senior team, to others who ensure that information flows freely throughout the organisation. If there is a change from one extreme to the other, it clearly impact on the organizational culture.

One respondent commented that 'communication isn't that easy as it was before as the GM is talking to each and every team member and therefore they now all follow the "open door" policy and take their problems to the GM instead of the department head'. The GM in this property was using his communication style to create influence throughout the organisation but was ignoring the established communication lines. This led to dissatisfied department heads.

This could also be seen positively: 'it was not the GM anymore that decided who received the information. The new leader was more open-minded and so everybody was included and everybody got all information and maybe 90% of it they didn't need... before we didn't have this, there was filtering and people made mistakes because sometimes information was missing'.

The various GMs described, however, all seemed to change something in the communication flow of the hotel to which they were posted.

Timescale

When respondents were questioned on the ideal length of time for a GM to stay in a property, the majority thought that approximately 5 years would be the best period. This would allow the GM to understand the market, gain trust from owners and business partners, know the people and culture of the property but also think sufficiently long term. A shorter period was seen as not in the best interest of the people and the hotel as the GM only focuses on short-term wins without addressing the long term strategy and profitability of the property.

Conclusions

The research highlights that the leader indeed has an influence on the organizational culture of a hotel. The change in organizational culture seems to be linked mostly to the change in 'management style'. It is not evident that the GMs make a conscious decision to change the organizational culture. It is their style of communication, decision making, empowerment etc. which make that change happen. Much also depends on the success of the predecessor as it can make it impossible for a successor to measure up.

A disadvantage is created if the new GM does not understand or is not able to interpret the existing organizational culture. The respondents mentioned that a new GM would sometimes make certain changes which then would need to be reversed afterwards.

With the arrival of a new leader the organisation may also get a positive boost as the person comes in highly motivated and can use their position to spread optimism, reinforce certain expected behaviours and give a sense of direction, harmony, confidence through speeches, work floor get-togethers and inspirational actions.

Corporate officers who are in charge of the succession planning of GMs should be aware of the disruption leadership changes can cause to the team members and the organizational culture. Specific attention should be given to the period referred to as 'stand still' i.e. the period between the departure of the predecessor and the arrival of the successor. This period ought to be kept as short as possible, in order to avoid delay on projects, cause anxiety amongst team members or the missing of commercial opportunities. A general anxiety is created when the incumbent GM announces his departure. Both the incumbent as well as his successor should be aware of this. Throughout the period of handover both GMs need to ensure that current projects continue without losing traction.

This research further suggests that adequate time and money needs to be spent on defining the leadership traits and management style for each GM. At each change of GM, considerable analysis should be undertaken to ensure the most appropriate GM is transferred to a new property to either maintain the existing culture (if successful) or to change and adapt the culture to the new strategy if this is needed.

GMs should be trained to learn and understand their influence on the organizational culture and how this culture, if used wisely, can help them to improve financial performance. GMs should be professionals in analysing the organizational culture and understand the benefits of a strong and positive culture. They should be aware which culture fits best to the organisation to deliver the desired strategy. To be able to create the ideal culture, GMs should be taught how a professional change management program can be applied. Such training should be part of the GMs learning and development training.

The recommendations are for the General Managers to focus on communication, trust, respect for the past and organizational culture change management. Each GM should understand the existing organizational culture and only make changes if this benefits the strategy of the hotel. The GMs should promote a strong and positive culture to increase staff retention, promote entrepreneurship, personal development etc. If a change is needed at all, then such a transformation to the organizational culture should be supported by a professional change methodology. Particular focus during this process ought to be given to comprehensive communication throughout the organization to limit anxiety and instability. From the research it becomes apparent that communication can never be enough and this is especially true during a period of change. Team members and management teams should be involved from the beginning, and the GM should create a compelling vision for the future and explain why the change is necessary. Simply changing things without an overall strategic approach will leave team members feeling dissatisfied and inadequate.

Finally, GMs should also be sensitive to team members who have been performing well over a number of years and are experiencing, once more, a GM change after which they will need to prove themselves again. During the period of change and in order to re-enforce the new desired behaviour, GMs need to create incentives to reward those team members that have adapted to the new organizational culture. This should help to create as soon as possible the new "Equilibrium".

Developing an Effective Hospitality Leadership Strategy for Generation Y – the Millennial

●

By Angela Vickers

Chief Executive, Apex Hotels

Angela Vickers BAcc MSc CA, Chief Executive Officer of one of the UK's leading independent groups of 4-star hotels. Edinburgh based Apex Hotels, own and operate nine contemporary-styled, city centre hotels located in London, Edinburgh, Glasgow and Dundee. A further 177 bedroom hotel and conference facility is under development in Bath, opening in summer of 2017.

Angela studied accountancy at Glasgow University (1986-89) joining KPMG Glasgow and was admitted to the Institute of Chartered Accountants Scotland in 1992. She subsequently joined Stakis Hotels and Leisure Group eventually running the Finance Shared Service Centre.

After nine years in the hotel sector, with Stakis Hotels then laterally Hilton Hotels, in 2002 Angela joined telecoms company Damovo as Finance Director for its corporate services division but returned to the hotel industry joining Apex Hotel as Finance Director before being promoted to Managing Director in 2005, 14 months after joining the business. Angela was appointed to CEO in January 2015.

Angela is Deputy Chair and Trustee of the charity HIT Scotland and a Trustee of the Springboard UK Charity.

Generation Y is one of the main sources of the hospitality workforce and is predicted to make up more than one quarter of the UK workforce by 2025. This generation displays a combination of unique traits; they think creativity, work collaboratively and are prolific in the use of technology.

Hospitality businesses generally rely on the younger labour pool to staff frontline positions. These frontline positions have a high level of customer interaction and service delivery, two important factors which can drive competitive edge and customer satisfaction. It is therefore important that hospitality HR practices pay cognizance to this emerging leadership pipeline.

The traditional hospitality leadership framework may not fit the unpredictable and fast paced environment that exists today. Emerging leaders are said to be ill prepared to take command in the future due to the unique set of circumstances that will evolve in relation to the multi-generational and diverse workforce, rapid technological developments and uncertain economic landscape.

Previous Research

Academic literature provides a valuable insight into Generation Y and through trait analysis it becomes clear that this generation is so different to those before. It is also recognised that social and economic changes are dictating that future leaders will need to bring new skills into the workplace as well as mastering old ones. This is compounded by the issue of engagement and retention of Generation Y within hospitality as they are prone to job hopping and seeking new challenges. To establish a robust and sustainable hospitality leadership pipeline the industry must first improve attraction and retention practices.

Generation Y, due to their sheer size, have the potential to shape every life stage that they enter. They were raised by parents who nurtured and lavished attention, in a secure and safe family environment. Millennials grew up in a time of economic prosperity, stable divorce rates and fewer siblings. They were taught to make their own choices, ask questions, participate in groups and teams and everyone was a winner. They have also lived during times of great economic uncertainty, terrible natural disasters such as Pakistan earthquakes, Indian Ocean tsunamis, Hurricane Katrina and world terrorism including 9/11. They therefore place value on life and self-fulfillment. As a result they place greater importance on time spent with the family than their predecessors. A study in the United States revealed that only 12-13% of Gen Y are work centric and 50% are family centric compared to 22% of baby boomers being work centric and only 41% family centric (Solnet & Hood 2010). They matured immersed in technology, hence the alternative moniker 'digital native' coined by Prensky (2001b). Prensky was referring to the fact that Millenials 'speak' fluently the language of computers, video games, social networks and the Internet. Multi-tasking comes naturally and 30 hours can be crammed into a 7 hour day (Millwood, 2007). They operate in a 24/7 virtual world using the mobile platform to stay connected and access unlimited data. Hershatter and Epstein (2010) state bluntly that Millennials are simply 'wired differently' than individuals from previous generations.

Generation Y think creativity, are problem solvers and collaborators. They look for greater flexibility in work, seeking a work life balance; they want work that really matters to them and has a sense of social responsibility and eco-awareness (Dries et al 2008, Hewlett et al 2009, Kowske et al 2010). They expect two way free flowing communication and are not intimidated by rank or position. Myers and Sadaghiani (2010) describe how millennials can bring disruption to traditional organizations but also point out that the benefits of adopting their collaborative behaviours can revitalize organizations. Generation Y have an innovative style and creativity of thought, good ingredients for a 'think tank' environment. They will not engage optimally if they are asked to sit at a desk for eight hours a day in a call centre cubicle. Work needs to be stimulating and therefore adjustments need to be made in the workplace, allowing them to work in different ways (Buchanon 2010, Gilbert 2011). Such adjustments include breaking tasks down into bite sized assignments, don't just explain the task but explain the what, why and how. Superiors should provide short and pertinent feedback at regular intervals, frequent deadlines are required to create a sense of urgency and genuine praise and gratitude should be expressed. Annual appraisals or semi-annual job reviews are insufficient to keep the millennials motivated. Provide checklists on how they can improve with specific suggestions and unambiguous feedback. Individual appreciation is required; this is not a 'one size fits all' generation. Generation Y respond to leaders not to micro managers, leaders who are passionate, engaging, inventive, entertaining and fun. Job sharing, job rotation, special assignments, remote or flexible working arrangements, authorized absences for volunteer working should be encouraged and adopted by employers. Their energy and enthusiasm they bring should be harnessed and nurtured by management.

So absorbing all of these traits and qualities of Gen Y and comparing them to the characteristics of the hospitality industry there is an obvious incongruence. The negative aspects of hospitality employment, in particular Hotels, were highlighted in various studies performed by Wood (1997). Where long unsocial working hours, low pay, menial tasks, low status, high staff turnover were citied. This is augmented with findings by Karatepe & Kilie (2007) of work-family conflict, Knox and Wood (2005) revealing employment strategies driven by cost reduction and Haynes and Fryer (2000) observing autocratic management styles with poor communication. Visit Scotland/George Street Research (2002) corroborated this image by identifying that although careers in the hospitality industry were thought to be challenging and interesting, they were also blighted with long hours, low pay and repetitive work. The current traditional hospitality environment appears inadequate to allow Generation Y, as the main workforce pool, the opportunity to thrive, prosper and deliver exceptional customer service.

It is evident that the hospitality industry needs to adjust to accommodate the new wave of Gen Y workers. Not only adjust, but positively re-enforce the congruent characteristics that are in alignment with Generation Y aspirations. Hospitality offers exceptional fast track career progression to those willing to work hard and commit to the industry, it also bestows responsibility to those willing and ready to accept the challenge from relatively early stages of employment. Team working and collaboration are highly desirable features of hospitality as is the opportunity for world travel given the highly mobile nature of the skills involved in this burgeoning industry.

Recruitment and retention have long been identified as one of the hospitality and tourism industry's biggest challenges (Powell and Wood, 1999). The labour turnover rate across the hospitality and tourism sector is 20% compared to a UK industry average of 15%. Turnover is already a concern with Generation Y, so much so that a new term was created to describe the issue; 'retention deficit disorder' (Johnson and Lopes 2008). If Generation Y consider themselves not to be advancing quick enough or are undervalued they will leave and look for alternative employment (Barron et al 2007).

In order to improve Generation Y's employer loyalty, hospitality has to be perceived as a long term valid career option. All too frequently it is used as temporary employment by graduates waiting on relevant jobs to become available in their chosen field of study in other industries or as a 'second' job to supplement main income or on a casual basis by students to earn money whilst studying. Rarely is it seen in the UK as vocational employment. Yet in a study carried out by Barron et al (2007) undergraduate hospitality students 'believed that if they made personal sacrifices and work hard early on in their careers it will pay off in the future'. Kerslake (2005) maintains that Gen Y can demonstrate loyalty and dedication provided they can also achieve their own personal goals. If they can't then they will vote with their feet and move on elsewhere.

Current Research Findings

The research was based on a programme of interviews with representatives of the following groups: senior hospitality leaders; Gen Y hospitality emerging leader forum group members; and non-hospitality senior leaders one to one interviews.

Firstly combining the output from these interviews with the academic literature, a matrix can be produced of the most desirable skills required to lead effectively:

Self-motivation/ discipline	Resourcefulness	Ethics & Integrity	Flexibility
Effective communication	Leading employees	Awareness of customer needs	Leading from the front / by example
Learning agility	Straightforwardness and composure	Time Management	Understanding of Branding
Self-awareness	Building and mending relationships	Speaking with Impact	People/ social skills
Adaptability/ versatility	Doing whatever it takes	Commitment to quality	Influencing

The project research also pointed out that an effective leadership program should be supplemented with workshops on how to maintain energy levels, better achieve a work life balance and maintain a healthy lifestyle. There may also be a need for the development of skills required to deal with leading a multi-generational and a multi-cultural workforce.

Referring to the specific Gen Y characteristics the research suggested the following ways in which the hospitality industry could start to maximize the potential of Generation Y.

Flexible working

Gen Y seeks time out to pursue hobbies and charitable works. Although Hotels are 24/7, and 365 days a year, better working practices should be adopted with no split shifts, enforcing 40 hour weeks, provide days in lieu for extra shifts worked, encourage better rostering practice and not take advantage of employees. Companies such as Marks and Spencer, John Lewis and RBS all have prominent CSR policies and actively encourage workforce participation. Many in Gen Y feel it is important that employers offer extended leave opportunities, and over half of these who take temporary leave use the time to explore passions or volunteer. A significant number of Gen Y value flexible working options, including preferring to work remotely. Hotel companies should offer sabbaticals, match charity fund raising activities, accommodate requests for remote working etc.

Collaboration

Hospitality offers an ideal environment for collaboration across functions, across hotels and for global organizations, across countries. Such collaboration exists in Marks and Spencer, RBS and IHG. Leadership groups were brought together to solve communication issues with customers and staff at M&S. RBS through the Pilotlight scheme collaborates with charities for mutually beneficial objectives. IHG provides another example with their 'Leaders Lounge' which is an intranet site, updated daily with interesting leadership articles, case studies, Harvard modules and interactive blogs. The site is accessed by leaders in training and existing leaders across the world as a social media interactive learning tool.

Challenge

Gen Y like to work out the best way to do a job, either on their own or with a team. They are great 'think tank' material. They won't settle with the status quo until all avenues have been investigated. Managers need to welcome this fresh way of thinking and factor in 'exploration' time and utilise their propensity to resolve business issues.

Techno savvy

This generation has never been without computers or access to information at the touch of a keyboard. They have their own websites and they continually customize and filter the plethora of online information and knowledge they are bombarded with. Hospitality companies could make better use of this skill by involving Gen Y in company social media activity, website development and user acceptance testing, digital distribution and keeping pace with technological advances.

Sense of urgency and immediacy

A year is a long time in the life of a Millennial and 2 years just a vision. They will want to know what they can learn today, be rewarded with today, tasked with today. Hospitality employers should increase project work and break down larger initiatives into smaller tasks where progress can be frequently recognized. They should eradicate policies which have been in place for years that prevent young talent from forging ahead and optimizing their potential.

Increasing responsibility

Gen Y love to prove themselves as an effective employee, they want to grow and be trusted. Reward accomplishments and jobs well done by increasing responsibility appropriately, this will keep motivation and contribution high. Provided the appropriate 'safety nets' are in place to catch Gen Y if should they fall, hospitality should not be afraid of giving immediate responsibility.

Need constant feedback/recognition

Don't wait for bi-annual or annual performance evaluations. Managers should constructively feedback daily, accentuate the positive and re-route back on track immediately. Give praise and recognition and this does not always have to be in a monetary format. Expose the leaders to hierarchy; ask them to present the results of their project work to Senior Management.

High expectations of employers

Be alert to their needs, get to know them as individuals, take time to explain the company mission, vision and values and explain how this may match to their own standards and ethics. Gen Y value close attention from their mentors and superiors. This is further re-enforced by trait theory where they like to be looked after by parental figures in a structured and value led environment.

Creative energy

Gen Y is brimming with creativity, they need variety – projects, training and development, social activities. If engagement levels are high, this should reduce the 'free agency' tag associated with this highly mobile workforce. Gen Y flourishes in a Project environment. As evidenced through the non-industry research, interactive project work plays a major role in banking and retail leadership development programs.

Prefer structure & direction

Gen Y are easily bored, they are used to multi-tasking but haven't been formally taught to time manage. They flight from one task to another. They will need coaching in how to better structure themselves, plan daily tasks and handle interruptions and moving deadlines. Provide realistic estimates of how long projects are likely to take and make it clear that leadership development does not happen overnight but must go through its proper course. As suggested by academic research assigning a mentor would greatly assist with this coaching. The research also pointed out that an effective leadership program should be supplemented with workshops on how to maintain energy levels, better achieve a work life balance and maintain a healthy lifestyle.

Emerging leaders should be trusted to hold positions of responsibility from the start of their training. The number of menial tasks should be reduced and low skilled tasks replaced with dynamic project work, leading small teams and making decision that actually impact the business. The following table combines academic and research findings and extends this thinking to further match Gen Y characteristics with working practices that employers can adopt to better engage and retain this generation;

Suggested Employer Strategies to Retain Millennials	
Career path	Clearly defined from entry, key milestones identified at regular intervals, supported by documented training program (rotational
Reward and Recognition	Respect, regular positive feedback / praise, internal promotion, incentive awards
Autonomy	Valued opinion, listened to, recognized and defined levels of responsibility.
Environment	Open door policy, brainstorming, Q&A sessions, participative
Diversity	Working parties which are cross functional, cross generational, international
Social interaction	'Outside office' social events, establish emerging leader organizations, encourage networking
Coaching / Mentoring	2 way or reverse mentoring with respected peer. Ask how they wish to be coached.
Ethics / Corporate Social Responsibility	Encourage voluntary working and offer paid leave. Be culturally ethical, consistent and transparent.
Working hours	Flexible working hours, portable workstations. Conducive to work/life balance.
Structure	Rules and policies, set boundaries on dress code, internet usage, mobile usage, meeting etiquette, business communication. Apply consistently.

Suggested Employer Strategies to improve Gen Y retention

In conclusion, is the Hospitality industry prepared for the arrival of the Gen Y Leader and is GenY adequately prepared to lead? Generation Y is unique and brings a fresh set of strengths. It would be foolish not to harness these strengths that can inject creativity into the hospitality industry. Pierre Gergis, Millennial and Business Transformation Consultant at IBM quotes;

"Millennials are not used to taking little steps and gradually wading into an ocean of knowledge; we're accustomed to diving in head first, rapidly adjusting, taking ownership of our successes and failures. We are a generation with a new work ethic and tremendous potential, given the resources and scope of a large corporation. That young people all over the world are creating brands and technologies that challenge and overshadow decades old institutions -- this start-up revolution -- is evidence enough of the great power of Millennial thinking. So rather than getting caught up in our youth and asking how we can be made more compatible to the work needed of us, I urge new questions to be asked, and innovative new work to open up. Integrate us correctly, and we Millennials can make corporate elephants dance."

Talent Management in the Hospitality Industry

By Torsten Pinter

General Manager of a Private Luxury
Oberwaid Hotel, St. Gallen

Torsten Pinter has worked in the Hospitality industry for over 25 Years and for the past 9 Years as General Manager of various Swissotel´s including China, Thailand and Switzerland. He recently moved on from his position in Swissotel and is currently the General Manager of a private luxury Hotel with private Clinic in St. Gallen called Oberwaid. Starting his early career as a baker and pastry chef, Torsten moved quickly into the Hospitality industry as an Executive Pastry chef but focused soon thereafter on hotel management starting as a trainee and ultimately making hotel management his career and passion. He is personally involved in several charitable organizations such as Kiwanis and World Vision and one of his personal aims is to complete a part time PhD within the next 5 years.

This chapter seeks to explore the nature of talent management, as experienced by leaders in the international hotel industry, with the aim of creating a policy framework that can help in the planning and development of talent management in hospitality organizations. According to Srinivasan (2011), there are two aspects to talent management: retaining and developing the talent of high performers and harnessing the talent of average and even under-performers. Clearly, for the success of an organization it is essential that both the high and the average performer receive equal attention. However, by treating higher performers in the same way as everyone else, one may risk losing the truly talented in the end.

Previous Research – Understanding and managing talent

Most CEOs consider talent management as a fundamental strategic objective (PWC, 2013). However, despite significant industry and academic interest, the understanding of the concepts of talent and talent management remains underdeveloped, with no generally accepted definitions (Collings and Mellahi, 2009). Thus, managing talent remains a difficult exercise for organizations, which struggle to plan and develop appropriate and effective talent management programs (PWC, 2013).

There is extensive evidence that employees who perceive that they receive support from their organization are less likely to consider leaving. Therefore one can argue that an employee's decision to stay or leave is influenced by their subjective appreciation of the value and usefulness of the support received from the organization, rather than by the existence or effectiveness of certain practices.

Implementing talent management effectively should result in an improved recruitment rate, a lower turnover rate and increased employee engagement. Church and Silzer (2014) explain that the understanding of the potential that lies within the organization is still one of the major points a company has to focus on, as companies still differ in their definitions of potential. Many senior executives continue to assess future potential employees based on either current performance or their own personal perspective and success story (the "like me" phenomena), which may or may not be grounded in what is needed for the future of the business.

As business grows more volatile and complex, it ushers in a new era of talent spotting. It is no longer enough for your employees and leaders to have the right skills, you need to hire people with the potential to learn and develop. Potential is harder to recognize than competence, so look for motivation, curiosity, and insight (Fernàndez-Aràos, 2009)

Church and Silzer (2011) explain that as different positions require different forms of potential raises the question of whether there are common components of potential across these specialized talent groups or whether they are very distinct. If there are some differences, then organizations need to ask themselves what type of potential they are looking for. Can an effective leader be equally successful in all situations or are there specialized leadership skills required for different functions or business situations.

McDonnell (2011) explains how in the recent past, there has been a shift towards the use of competency profiles in identifying talent. Supporting a good balance between intuitive and analytical selection of talent, Kesler (2002) argues that many executives believe people selection is an intuitive task, and most senior leaders rate their own intuition very highly. The fact is that assessment is a skill that must be developed. Once the tools and skills are mastered, they are transferable, but when an executive joins a new management team, standards must be re-calibrated.

McCauley and Wakefield (2006) explain that Human Resources departments can set the stage for success by hiring and training capable employees. However, developing those personnel into dynamic, motivated, long-term participants in the company's processes must be the responsibility of all management, from CEO to floor supervisor. The talent management process includes workforce planning, talent gap analysis, recruiting, staffing, education and development, retention, talent reviews, succession planning, and evaluation.

By analysing where talent is missing and from where talent can be sourced, firms ensure the selection and employment of the right workers that are fitting for the vacant positions.

As soon as the pool of potential and talented workers is established, it is necessary to first define who of the internal candidates can and needs to be supported and given talent development and who needs to be brought in from the outside. McDonnell (2011) argues that this situation has led some to question whether a 'war for talent' (Michaels et al., 2001) has been replaced by a 'war on talent'.

Firms that fill open positions with people who exactly match the job specification are selling their firms short. They are hiring for right now instead of the long term. Blakely(2013) suggests building a talent pool that is as nimble and dynamic as your company. By doing so, the firm can guarantee a steady flow of talented workers that are ready to take on the vacant key positions within the firm, in order to assure its long-term success.

Despite the rising unemployment rate in many countries, workforce demographics still point to critical skills (talent) shortages. In other words, strategic anchoring of talent management has never been more important because an organization's talent will be one of the principal guideposts in turning the downturn into long-term organizational sustainability and success.

Current Study Findings

The implementation of today`s available talent management processes and strategies are relatively new. Comparing today`s strategies and processes with the known Human Resources processes of the past, it shows that managing talent was not recognized and organized in a systematic way. This chapter reports on interviews with 20 senior managers in the hospitality industry who are involved in managing talent and employed by a company that has a talent management program.

Talented individuals were mostly identified and developed (often subconsciously) by managers working within the operational level, such as a headwaiter grooming one of his apprentices over the years to become assistant restaurant manager.

The career development was purely based on learning by doing without any support through individual development plans.

Some general managers argue that talent is something which comes naturally, which one is born with.

"Talent for me is something that is imbedded in the person, where you have certain strength, you have certain talents that you cannot be taught, you cannot learn."

Some argue that everybody has some kind of talent which can be useful for their career and eventually for the organization which employs them.

"Everybody has a talent, but not every talent is important for the industry."

Others see it as a combination of the talent that one is born with, as well as the environment that further shapes the talent of an individual are of equal importance. If these two factors are not in harmony, it could potentially jeopardize the development of a talented person.

"For me, talent is something we are born with, that still needs to be developed and nurtured over the years, in order to reach its full potential."

If a doorman, for example, has the ability to identify returning guests and greet them by name, he will contribute to a guest experience that can create a high level of customer satisfaction.

However, this ability does not guarantee that he will be able to move up to a leadership role, as this role may require a different skill-set and a higher level of talent.

Some of the general managers interviewed told me that they knew of cases where colleagues are not aware of their talent and do not believe in their strengths. And in these cases, it makes it really difficult or even impossible to help these people develop.

"Some people do not understand their real talent and strength, and therefore focus on the wrong positions within an organisation.

Thus, there is a strong consensus among the interviewees that only a very small percentage of those with high potential will ever make it into a leadership position because the required talent for this level is very rare.

Another important aspect is to distinguish between those with high potential talent who are specialists from those who are generalists. Not every talented person has the required leadership potential to manage units/organizations. Specialists have the potential to be in charge of important key positions, such as IT, Accounting or Revenue Management. Generalists are those who possess the capability of maintaining an overview across multiple roles and departments, however, they may not be as in-depth as specialists in the respective departments.

"I think specialists and leadership have to go together, but leadership does not necessarily have to go together with specialists."

Though the interviewed GMs define talent in a similar way as the organizations they work for, the latter also include certain expectations and selection criteria, such as specific skill-sets and the mobility of the individual in their definition. The selection criteria seem to be based on the different strategies of an organization. For example, the leadership skills and know-how required to grow a luxury hotel portfolio is different from that necessary to develop a business hotel portfolio. However comparing the data it seems that most interviewees find it difficult to identify how their respective companies define talent. A possible explanation for this is that companies tend to mainly focus on measurable core competencies, as well as past experiences which can be substantiated by diplomas and certificates and tend to focus less on personality traits, dedication, service-mindedness and passion.

"The company identifies talent in key members or colleagues with natural skills that can be developed for the benefit of the company." - Kevin Furrer

When talking about the required core competencies, it was interesting to learn that most General Managers agreed that the people who make the difference in our industry have very good communication skills, a passion to deliver service, the strength to analyse situations quickly, and know how to solve problems (short- and long-term) and most importantly love their profession, even looking at the hospitality profession as their calling and not just a job.

"The main competency for me is the ability to speak and to listen, especially listen to people, and then have the ability to analyse what these people exactly have to say and what needs to be done, and make a plan out of that."

"I think you naturally need people, who are difficult to find, basically, it is for them – I don't want to say a hobby, it's sort of like a violinist who loves to play an instrument and becomes, later on, a great musician. People who love to be with people, who love to have challenges and overcome them."

A few of the interviewees explained the need to have an academic degree as one of the core competencies, arguing that the risk to select the wrong candidate is smaller when considering candidates with academic degrees as against those without.

When asking who is the driving force behind successful talent management, it became apparent that the leaders of the organization need to take the lead and be fully responsible in assuring a successful implementation, ongoing consistency, as well as continuous improvement of this important strategy. Without the support of the leader it is extremely difficult to cascade the idea of talent management throughout all levels of the organization.

"Surround yourself with talented people for the success of the organization."

"Talent management is the responsibility of the executive team in cooperation with Human Resources."

To identify and select talented people, we need to have leaders/managers in place who have the ability to identify high potential candidates and are objective in their selection process, not allowing themselves to be influenced by political or personal reasons, especially for management and leadership positions. Great leaders have the ability to mentor their colleagues by identifying, acknowledging and developing their strengths.

"It certainly helps to make a selection, but I think, as an executive, you need to have the talent yourself to detect talent in other people. You look at them, you see how they talk to you, you look into their eyes, their demeanour, their body language and you will know somebody is burning for the job and they really want to have it."

From a process perspective, talent management includes the following three steps: (1) identifying the talent, (2) developing the talent according to their strengths and (3) providing future possibilities within the company, not only for its own benefit, but for that of the individual, as well.

In most hotels, talent management has existed for a long time but without a specific process in place. Most hiring, identifying and selecting of the high potential candidates (out of the available talent pool) was done intuitively. Supporting systems and strategies have now been implemented and embraced. These tools are helping to select the right candidates for the right positions. However, most General Managers agree that the final call to groom a candidate for a particular position, is based on a gut-feeling which comes with many years of experience within the industry.

"We have tools available which support the hiring process of candidates, but the final decision I will make based on my gut feeling."

An interesting debate occurs with regard to whether talent management should fall under the umbrella of Human Resources.

"In my opinion, talent management should form its own department. Maybe it should be turned around - Human Resources management should rather be part of talent management."

The data has revealed that the present situation does not allow the Human Resources department to incorporate talent management activity successfully due to a lack of resources and knowledge.

If these gaps in resources and knowledge are bridged, Human Resources could eventually assist in the process of managing talent, but the full ownership of talent management demands the engagement and responsibility of the entire management team. For the success of any organization, not only the engagement but also the accountability of a professional talent management process is crucial.

Building on this theory, Kempinski Hotels and Resorts has separated the Human Resources responsibilities into 3 key pillars:
- People Service (HR Administration)
- Training (Training Manager)
- Talent Management (responsibility of the leadership)

People services are only doing the administration processes. They're not involved in interviews, in talent decision, nor in anything which is related to leadership.

While conducting the interviews, several issues came to the surface regarding the barriers and challenges. Firstly, there are generational issues that outline notable differences between Generation X and Y. Generation Y does not seem to have a long-term vision that they consult when taking career steps. This makes it very difficult to establish development and career planning. In addition, it discourages the management from investing time and money in this generation which is very important for the industry.

"Having workers leave and never hiring them back is old-school, the Generation Y doesn't work like that anymore." - Gerhard Struger

Leaders occasionally fail to distinguish between efficiency and effectiveness. The hazard is that this could affect the motivation of the individual and eventually snowball through the team, meaning there is a clear difference between a hardworking and a talented person.

The main challenge is the lack of a long-term development and career plan. A long-term development plan needs to assure the required time to groom the high potential candidate and to provide job opportunities for the different career steps. The benefit for the employer is two-fold. Not only will the employer maintain the employee, but they will also benefit from the increased knowledge and experience of their employee.

"Management needs to dedicate more time to people development - be it coaching, training or planning. Where do we want to see young talent in three, five or even ten years from now and how can we guide them to get there." - Michael Smithuis

If job opportunities within the organization are limited, some of the interviewees suggested exploring working with selected properties of the competition. This not only helps the employer branding but also provides a future opportunity to retain the employee with an expanded horizon.

"If I cannot help him within the group, then and quite frankly it is sometimes very difficult within our organization. What I do is I place them with our competition. ."

Talent management, as the identified core strategy, starts with hiring and developing people but is a continuous process. One of the greatest issues is open communication within the team and with the corporate level of the organization. Creating and implementing a talent management system which empowers and supports colleagues in thinking out of the box and being creative for the benefit of the organization will make the difference.

"Well, in the case of talent management, you can take a very academic approach, but I think it's all about simplicity. It's about talking to the people, finding out what they want to do, what do we see, what can they do and what potential is there and filling that gap and bringing the people where they need to go."

Ultimately, the approach to manage talent calls for a more flexible but organized system. Thus, to attract different generations, work flexibility, personal freedom and work-life balance is a must. Retaining talent goes far beyond posting a creative job advertisement. Talent management also shapes the perception of the working environment that the organization provides to its employees, which can be called employee branding or employer attractiveness.

"We have to get better at it, because it's the future of the industry."

Hospitality is an industry where every individual contributes to the ultimate goal of meeting and exceeding guest expectations. By doing so, it will allow an organization to pace itself ahead of its direct competitors. In light of the above, it is needless to say that people and managing them are the components that contribute to the success and in some cases even the survival of an organization. Organizations should assure an ongoing and long-term (3-8 years) professional development of their future leaders.

It may be beneficial to have a Talent Management Committee. The selection of team members for the committee should bring together decision makers and influencers from within the team. The Talent Management Committee should focus on the following six important areas:

- Forecast supply and demand of talent within the organization that supports the company's programs and goals.
- Identify the talent from the available potential candidates and further select the high potentials from the pool of potential candidates.
- Implement career development plans based on the strengths of the individual high potentials.
- Pro-actively establish a tailored, long-term development plan based on the strengths of the individual. This plan needs to clearly outline the steps that are required to obtain the desired goal.
- Provide educational possibilities and additional benefits to further increase the retention rate, and reduce the turnover ratio.
- Evaluate procedures and technology solutions to improve the data management of the candidates.

Employer Branding and its Role Within the Hospitality Industry

By Richard Ellison

General Manager, Hilton DoubleTree, Dundee

Originally from York, **Richard** started his hotel career at the age of 13 working as a kitchen porter at the Churchill Hotel in York. Moving to Dundee in 1996 as Assistant Manager at the Swallow Hotel he in 2001 took a position at Gleneagles Hotel, Perthshire eventually being promoted to Event Operations Manager.

After 5 years at Gleneagles, Richard took a role as GM at the Columba Hotel Inverness and thereafter as GM at Norwood Hall Hotel, Aberdeen. Having joined the 5* Old Course Hotel in 2008 as the Resident Manager, he was awarded the Caterer and Hotelkeeper magazine Hotel Catey award for the Food & Beverage Manager of the Year 2008. In 2010 Richard helped start an events business returning shortly thereafter as General Manager of the Landmark Hotel in Dundee during which he was awarded company GM of the year 2012 and commended by the Scottish Hotel Awards. The hotel was awarded city hotel of the year for three consecutive years and Scotland's brand hotel of the year in 2013. In 2013 Richard led the rebrand of the hotel to the Hilton branded DoubleTree by Hilton Dundee.

Since 2005 a significant increase in interest within 'employer branding' has continued to grow following the purported introduction by Ambler and Barrow in 1996 as an activity for human resources teams.

Despite the growth within the topic, there is still a large amount of doubt about the definition and success of engaging an employer branding strategy within organisations. Part of this ambiguity is the topic crosses a number of HR activities such as communications, recruitment, training, performance management etc.

Within the hotel sector it is generally accepted that retaining employees and managing employee turnover are the biggest problems facing hotel operators (Main 1998).

The industry in general continues to have one of the highest turnover rates across industries because of wages, shift schedules and social perceptions of entry level jobs (Hurst 1997).

The negative impact of this influences employee training costs, quality performance, rating from customers and employee job satisfaction.

Retention of employees is also affected due to the factors above and an employee's intention to leave the industry has been found to be directly related to the level of employee job satisfaction (Vallen, 1993; Hackes and Hamouz, 1996).

The aim of this chapter is to further understand how different companies within the one hotel industry engage their employees to improve employee satisfaction and therefore increase the likelihood of employee retention, drive productivity and increase quality of service.

Past Research

In the first documented reference to the subject, Ambler and Barrow (1996: p8) defined employer branding as;

'The employer brand as the package of functional, economic and psychological benefits provided by employment and identified with the employing company.

The main role of the employer brand is to provide a coherent framework for management to simplify and focus priorities, increase productivity and improve recruitment, retention and commitment'

Similarly the Conference Board (2001) wrote, 'the employer brand establishes the identity of the firm as an employer. It encompasses the firm's value system, policies and behaviours toward the objectives of attracting, motivating, and retaining the firm's current and potential employees'.

There is a three step strategy in the creation of an employer brand:
1. Developing a value proposition
2. Market the value proposition to potential employees
3. Internal marketing of the value proposition

A value proposition reflects the organisation's culture, management style, qualities of current employees and the quality of the product or service. (Sullivan 2002).

Communicating the value proposition to potential employees is the more complicated and varied step within the process.

The external stakeholders include not only the potential employees themselves but also employment agencies and colleges.

The marketing of this proposition is intended to attract talent but must also support and promote the product or brand itself. In other words, whatever the 'attraction message' is, it must be truly representative of the brand itself. It is fundamental that the employer brand be consistent with all other branding efforts of the firm (Sullivan, 2004).

The final step in the process is the internal communication and marketing of the employer brand. This message carries the brand "promise" made to recruits into the firm and incorporates it as part of the organisational culture (Frook, 2001). The message should be a clear understanding of how employees should 'act' within the firm to demonstrate the values, culture and organisational goals set by the firm as promised to new recruits, sometimes described as 'walking the talk'.

Current Study Findings

The sample for this study was broken down into 3 target groups:
1. Hotel brand or hotel management company executives
2. Hotel general managers working in branded hotels managed by a hotel management company
3. Hotel employees working in branded hotels managed by a hotel management company

All subjects tentatively described their understanding of employer branding referring to the nature as being ambiguous. Culture was discussed as being a key part of employer branding with the senior executives discussing this in detail and making regular reference to it using terms such as a 'defined organisational culture' and 'strong employee engagement'.

The hotel general managers and hotel employees predominantly defined the term as 'how a business is perceived' and 'what the employees look and act like'.

The hotel management company representative further clarified the association with culture, in the context of employer branding, by describing the importance of the business leader (General Manager) within the hotel over the importance of the hotel brand above the front door stating "if we have the right leader in the business who lives and breathes our culture and mission, regardless of the hotel brand over the front door of the hotel, we believe that to be a good example of employer branding"

All of the general managers and executives believed that they operated an employer branding exercise within their hotels. Interestingly, out of the employees none of them believed that the hotel they worked in knowingly operated an employer brand or had been discussed with them at any stage.

The executives described the employer brand as 'essential' and 'was a collective term of HR practices and policies that was used to attract and retain new recruits', yet the general managers and employees all viewed it as a new concept that business were using to mainly attract new recruits with no reference to retention.

The gap in definition between groups was also highlighted when the discussions focused on values or rewards. Despite the executives commenting that whilst the rewards were a part of the employer brand and referred to them as 'hygienic items', this group felt that the term was more focussed on corporate values, beliefs and subsequent behaviours. The GMs and employees focused more on the aforementioned hygiene factors which included items such as pay, reward, development and employee benefits.

The researcher was keen to learn which organisational brands the subjects viewed as having a strong employer brand and why. The list included companies such as 'Apple, Nike, Google, Mövenpick Hotels, Hilton, Malmaison, IHG, McDonald's, and TGI Fridays'

The company that was named the most was McDonald's.

The subjects gave the reasons for McDonald's as a company with a clear employer brand because they had a clear understanding of 'What employees will do if they work there' and 'what it would be like to work there is clear because you can see it'.

Malmaison Hotels, TGI Fridays and Apple were mentioned because their external marketing to both customers and future employees were of a similar design and message.

One hotel brand described their strong employer brand as one based on values, clear mission statement, clear and proud description of their history and quantifiable culture. It summarised its employer brand as focussing on 3 key areas:
- Values
- Development
- Reward

Each new employee has a clear understanding of what each of these three opportunities means to them at job advert stage and this is re-iterated on induction. Existing employees also have access to an interactive and constantly refreshed training portal and brand intranet. Following their training and development, employees have the opportunity to view and apply for internal brand job vacancies around the globe through their job portal. This 'job board' also includes inspirational stories from recently promoted employees aimed at both future recruits and internal employees. The employee and friends and family travel scheme is something the brand value extremely highly in terms of employer branding both relating to attraction and retention. The brand have also introduced a new leadership initiative in the US which will migrate across to Europe in the near future. The initiative is called 'Every employee will have a great boss'. This is a very powerful promise to each and every employee and asks the employee the question 'Do you have a great boss?' The theory behind the campaign is to promote leadership behaviours and give employees the opportunity to give 360 degree feedback to their leaders in order to ensure they have a 'voice'. The brand clearly demonstrated a strong employer brand message and was thorough in its message that it speaks to both external and internal stakeholders whilst encapsulating the corporate brand message. It admitted that work was still to be done on post-employment to further understand exactly why people leave the brand, but rated themselves highly on items such as development and reward.

The hotel management company identified a different type of challenge for them in terms of employer branding. Their key challenge was the various messages it felt it had to give out to different stakeholders regarding their employer brand. These stakeholders included hotel owners, hotel brands, current employees and potential employees. The management company have recently introduced an employer brand strategy and at a recent general managers meeting requested input into brand messages for the HR and marketing team to formulate a more robust employer branding strategy. The management company felt that whilst it is very important to have a strong employer brand which will retain employees, they feel that they have work to do in terms of attraction.

They categorised employees working in their business from three groups:
1. Those that choose to work at the hotel because of geographical convenience (i.e. no relevance to brand or management company)
2. Those that choose to work at the hotel because of its brand (i.e. Hilton, Marriott, IHG)
3. Business leaders that choose to work with the management company because of their (management company) employer brand

Interestingly, where the brand and management company appear to differ is in the targeted recruitment approach. The employer brand from the management company is targeted at general managers and not directly at entry level employees. Referring back to an earlier comment made, the management company representative reiterated "if we have the right leader in the business who lives and breathes our culture and mission, regardless of the hotel brand over the front door of the hotel, we believe that to be a good example of employer branding"

Therefore this targeted approach is a distinct difference between the hotel brands and the hotel management companies. This approach was also echoed by the hotel general managers.

One of the respondents said "I would work for any brand of hotel as long as it was managed by the current management company".

The general managers also felt that the employer brand was stronger with the brands in terms of recruitment, development and employee attraction, however, could not implement the same positive culture that the management company could do due to sheer scale and loss of control.

For the hotel management company, one of the issues was that it was important for the customers within the hotel to not have the management company employer brand imposed on them too much as this may interfere with the branded employer brand message that the customer purchased. An example of this would be for a guest staying at a Crowne Plaza hotel (IHG brand) managed by a hotel management company. The hotel named brand takes precedent in the guests mind over the company that operate and run it.

One of the questions asked of the employees was 'Which company do see yourself working for? 3 out of the 4 named the hotel brand rather than the management company thus denoting a closer alignment to the brand than the management company for those employees.

Whilst the management company have a lesser structure to their employer brand message than that of the hotel brands they feel it offers more flexibility for their employees. One of the challenges for the company is how they get that marketing message across to both internal and external candidates across a variety of hotel brands each with different standards of performance, induction and brand promises.

The hotel brand said they experienced fewer issues with employer branding as they felt that their brand was strong and their cultural link between both the corporate brand and the employer brand was evident.

As the hotel brands operate more and more franchise agreements, the lack of control may bring in more challenges. Ultimately, this will be a key test for the strength of the brands as they step away from direct management of them and allow third parties to pick up their brand and the supporting structure.

Another issue highlighted was in relation to executing the employer brand message. Does the brand 'walk the talk' and transfer their recruitment message into fruition and reality once the candidate joins the organisation.

"It is easy to put together a great looking attractive recruitment advert promising rewards and development but if the reality is very different when a candidate joins the business it will have a negative impact on brand".

Organisations need to deliver on their messages so that there is a link between the marketing message be it to internal or external employees or the organisations consumers, the organisation must then be able to 'walk the talk' and demonstrate this through actions, behaviours, culture and values, thus making the employer brand as tangible as possible.

Through the interviews, the hotel management company executive talked about 'having the right leader' and if the hotel management company's employer brand message resonates and is promoted with him/her, then this should be sufficient for the message to be purposeful and achieve the benefits and aims it attempts to do.

The hotel brands must by their nature have a strong employer brand message. As their business becomes more asset light, it is imperative that one of the key USPs for the branded hotel is recognition, identity and loyalty both with its customers and employees. To have a competitive edge it needs to be: best in class in terms of benefits for the employees; easy to communicate across the globe and to various hotel management companies and audited regularly to ensure that the employer brand messages are alive and practiced within the hotels.

Attracting Hospitality Graduates

By Gerhard Struger

Regional Vice President, FRHI Hotels and Resorts

Gerhard Struger, a native of Austria, utilises his international knowledge and experience of the Travel and Hospitality industries to aid in the success of the Turkey & Eastern Europe Region for FRHI – Swissôtel, Fairmont and Raffles Hotels & Resorts. Having joined Swissôtel Hotels & Resorts in 1997 as Executive Assistant Manager in Istanbul he has since managed various Swissôtels around the world. Returning to Swissôtel The Bosphorus, Istanbul as General Manager in 2005 he was in 2007 appointed Regional Vice President Turkey & Eastern Europe. Gerhard Struger was included in the Hall of Fame for Special Achievements in the Tourism Industry from PATWA when Swissôtel Berlin won the Business Hotel of the Year Award in 2004 and received the Gold Medal for special Achievements by the Federal State of Upper Austria. He is a member of the Advisory Board of the Hotel Management Program at Ozyegin University in Istanbul, a board member of the Turkish Hotelier Association and the Chaine des Rotisseurs Turkey and a board member of the Swiss-Turkish Chamber of Commerce.

Nowadays, the pressure to treat colleagues with equal care and sensitivity as we do customers is greater than ever. Work-life balance is a repeating subject in forums and discussions as well as business strategies. Companies not providing a work-life balance will not attract the best colleagues into their work force. For the hotel sector this is a particularly difficult subject as a 24-hour/365-day business has challenges in maintaining loyalty with colleagues. Other industries that provide a regular work- life balance or

even partial or full work from home may be viewed as more attractive than a shift driven business. The objective of this chapter is to understand how employers in smaller hotel chains can develop and manage their brand and activities, to become more attractive to potential graduate employees, better align their strategy to the potential employees' personal motivations and career aspirations subsequently creating higher employee retention.

Previous Research

According to Sigler (Sigler 1999) "in a perfect world the productive employees are encouraged to stay within the organization and the non-productive poor performers are encouraged to leave." He suggests that companies will keep employees who are profitable to the company and who have a more positive influence on the company. However, Maxwell and Knox (2009) argues that focusing only on attributes related to the employee's role when recruiting, may not be sufficient. They suggest that employers should also try to increase the positive image within peer groups of potential future employers to increase the overall image and subsequently retention. They "... suggest that employees may seek to align their own views with other people who are in some way similar to themselves..."

This is also confirmed by a research conducted by Terjesen et al., (2007) with over 800 students, about the attractiveness of work places amongst various industries. The most important attribute, for both male and female students was – "to be employed by people with whom you feel you will have things in common".

A similar aspect is brought up by Solnet et al., (2008) when looking at the preferred attributes that an employer should be providing to the market. The ten most desired attributes were intrinsic ones and they argue that Generation Y in particular is looking for fun, involvement, training and development. They will be easier recruited and retained through exposure to meaningful projects and proper support.

In understanding why people want to work in hospitality, a study by Arnett et al., (2002) identified the importance of pride in the organization. Pride is influenced by job satisfaction, evaluation of managers/management and the organizational performance.

Mission and values are imperative to create this pride. Through those values, the company's brand image is defined. Communication both to internal and external customers is the next step – internal via human resources and public relations alongside external through advertising and public relations. Clarity in delivering the message is mandatory. Based on the communication a psychological contract is formed between the employer and the employee. The psychological contract is a perception of the working conditions and environment from the employee's perspective. (Miles and Mangold 2005)

There is a need to understand the changing nature of the new generation of employees. Generation Y is a fast moving generation and life time employment is not a consideration any longer, as was with earlier generations. They need a fast paced environment and will not wait until something is given to them. They would rather go out and get it. They are also more resistant to pressure and want quicker results, growth and empowerment.

In a focus group study by Barron, et al., (2007) amongst 25 level 3 and 4 hospitality students, the result was interesting insofar as they were not necessarily considering a long-term career in the branded hotel business, preferring in the long term to set up their own business. The negative aspects of branded hotels centred on poor pay and unsociable working hours. Also there was a perception of negative communications and unfair reward systems.

Customization of the work place to the needs of Generation Y graduates seems an important factor in improving retention and helping them on their career path. We have seen that this group, once entering the job market, enjoys learning by doing, a much more experimental style than the current management generation. Shaw (Shaw and Fairhurst 2008) suggests one way to overcome a potential knowledge gap is by mentoring and coaching programs that ease the way into the job market and up the career ladder. Coaching programs are available in a number of bigger organisations and have proven to be quite successful. Development programs should be flexible and adapted to the individual situation. Graduates should be able to move vertically and horizontally to enlarge their knowledge base and get a better understanding of the business.

Current Research

Two groups of hospitality students at a Swiss hotel school were invited to a focus group to discuss their employment plans. The students came from China, Japan, Vietnam, Russia, Ukraine, Slovakia, Portugal, Germany, North America and others.

The discussions started by looking at company size. It was generally agreed that to start with a smaller hotel company of say between 10 and 150 hotels rather than a very large chain is more beneficial to your career. You can see more and do more in a smaller company, you are more visible and can possibly grow faster. The important issue in the early stages of a career is to gain experience. Part of that experience seeking is also to hop around different work places. Later, when a certain career level has been reached, you should stay on for longer periods.

The Asian participants tended to be more interested in choosing an employer that they can be loyal to whereas the Eastern Europeans were generally more aggressive towards moving and growing, the quicker the better.

During this discussion the learning theme came up for the first time. It was important for students to gain experience and grow their own knowledge. This subject came up again and again. "It is growth that matters the most. Our expectation is (to) grow as professionals within a company."

For the fast paced Generation Y it is also necessary to provide enough learning opportunities and growth opportunities. It seems that graduates are geographically flexible and are happy to move, as long as they can gain an overall benefit.

It was found generally rewarding to live an international life, e.g. work in different parts of the world and get exposed to different cultures. "I have moved around in normal life and I think it is what I want to continue."

The students were aware of the fact that the industry is not very work – life balanced. The consensus was that once you move into this industry you understand that you work long and odd hours, especially in the early stages of your career. This was not considered to be unique to the hospitality sector. "... in whichever sector you start, you have to work hard: you have to prove that you can do the job. It doesn't matter if it is hospitality, accounting or whatever. You still have to work hard".

More senior positions give more flexibility and stability in terms of a work pattern. Working hard in the beginning pays back in promotion opportunities. When asked about becoming a CEO and if this was in their life plan, the groups, although divided, eventually found that this is not on the top of their list. Their lifestyle is more important!

Brand was considered important when developing your career, when working on your CV. But ultimately brand is less important when compared to work-life balance. The discussion again rolled around the subject of appreciation and quality of life. Some rather preferred to stay with non-branded employers or small independent companies and have a good life rather than be in a big brand and be unhappy. "… brand is more important for your CV, rather than for your future satisfaction. You need to feel comfortable and happy when you go to work. I think we want to work at where we are qualified, at a place where you can perform".

The big brands like Google, Coca Cola, Apple roused admiration, but they are not necessarily where students want to be.

Relationship, a sense of belonging, environment, recognition and motivation were of greater importance. "It is growth, it is motivation, recognition, opportunities. It is feeling like home, I guess".

Students were asked to describe their preferred workplace. The best work place, it was agreed, is the one that gives you a chance to learn across different departments and have regular appraisals from superiors and good feedback from guests. The main positive experience revolves around meeting new people, learning new things and making new experiences.

Conclusions

Students' expectations mainly rotate around the theme of learning, growing and gaining experience but also around lifestyle. Whereas brand has an influence on pride, for many students the intrinsic factors like recognition, experience, and teamwork were of higher importance than the brand.

To provide learning opportunities was one of the key priorities of every student interviewed. More than anything, this is a key criterion to attract people and a key opportunity to maintain employee loyalty. Fast track learning, providing assistance in career building, training programs, providing new experiences, meeting with new people and exploring new places across geographic regions were on the wish list of many.

Another important theme was revolving around emotional factors – emotional binding, a sense of belonging, value (feedback, evaluation, appraisal) and the company showing respect for the employee. Other factors that were of importance revolved around work-life balance. Respect for family life and providing a sustainable life are an issue. Where possible, companies should create jobs that are not fixed in starting and ending times, but where people can choose their working hours. Due to the nature of the business this may not be possible for all departments, but nevertheless the role of duty rosters may be coming to an end sooner rather than later. Also with technology many jobs can be done at home, as long as they are done. Career is important, but not at all costs. The Generation Y employee will not necessarily compromise their own life and lifestyle for a hospitality career.

Enhancing the Attractiveness of Entry Level Hospitality Jobs

●

By Jennifer Neil

Founder, Tallpoppies Scotland Ltd

Jennifer Neil has gathered over 25 years' national and international experience in the service, hospitality and tourism sectors. Her talent is in the interpretation and presentation of ideas. She is passionate about visitor experience (from her formative years spent in her family's hotel business) and helping organisations and businesses understand and engage with their visitors through effective brand expression.

Started in 2006, Jennifer's own hospitality and tourism consultancy agency, Tallpoppies has successfully delivered projects such as the £1.25m 'Tourism Intelligence Scotland', 'Listening to our Visitors' and 'Destination Development' initiatives for Scottish tourism. Tallpoppies built a reputation for developing innovative tourism initiatives to motivate and enable businesses and professionals to work creatively, collaboratively and with the visitor at the core.

Jennifer and her team also manage a portfolio of unique, individually designed serviced apartments in the West End of Edinburgh.

In addition to the Executive Masters in Hospitality and Tourism Leadership, Jennifer's academic career includes a BA (Hons) from Glasgow School of Art and a MSc in International Business and Japanese from Stirling and Saitama Universities.

The hospitality and tourism sector in the UK is one of the main employers of young people for entry level jobs and yet traditionally this industry has difficulty in finding the right people to fill its vacancies. This situation has deepened with the growth of the industry over the last 20 plus years.

The hospitality industry would seem to be an ideal choice for many young job seekers, as unlike many other industries, it has many diverse job roles, with opportunities for progression and for transferrable skills to be utilised across the sector. The industry can support a wide range of people from a wide range of backgrounds and educational achievements and can offer its workforce many life skill opportunities as well as technical ones. It really is an industry with something for everyone with career opportunities as diverse as; sales, marketing, customer service, cooking, health and beauty, construction, facilities management, design, IT and so on. It has been said that the hospitality industry might be viewed as 'a modern day army' which can offer a wide range of technical and social skills – many of which are transferable to other industries. So from fast food to five stars and everything in-between, this is an industry with a wealth of career possibilities – for people with the right kind of attitude and with a spirit to get ahead.

So if this industry is so appealing - why do skills shortages in hospitality remain so high? What are we doing to excite and inspire our young people to make a career in the industry and what do employers, schools and colleges do to encourage young people's continued learning in a sustainable way?

The aim of this chapter is to identify how education leavers (16-18 years) acquire the 'right' skills for entry level jobs in hospitality and how they are attracted into the industry in the first place.

Previous Research

There is clearly a sizeable opportunity within the hospitality industry for employment. To illustrate this vibrancy, between 2007 and 20012, it is reported that the number of budget hotel rooms alone in the UK grew by 35% and all predictions are that the budget market, as well as other markets is set to grow further (Springboard, 2012).

Yet against this optimistic outlook, there are many 'hard to fill vacancies' within the industry with the main reason for this, being the low number of applicants with the required skills, motivation, attitude or personality.

With the hospitality industry becoming more diverse, it follows that there is also a very diverse range of different employee profiles – each who are attracted to a particular style of business. A distinction should be made on the relative differences between 'back of house' job roles and 'front of house' job roles with regard to employer requirements. There will naturally be a greater emphasis on appearance and personality etc. for 'front of house' staff, but it would appear that increasingly 'back of house' staff are also being viewed in terms of company values and 'right fit'. For more forward thinking companies who pride themselves on customer service, the concept is explained to employees as either 'you are directly serving the customer' or 'indirectly serving the customer'. And so the requirement for 'back of house' staff then becomes not dissimilar to front of house staff, in needing to fit in with company values (of teamwork, integrity, respect for all and so forth). For the purposes of this study, the focus will be predominately on 'front of house' job roles but that is not to ignore 'back of house' roles for the reasons mentioned.

Regardless of the type of hospitality business, its people will always be the biggest challenge and also its greatest differentiator. As People 1st (2013 page 9) concludes, 'With rising expectations, increased competition and knowledgeable customers looking for both value for money and good quality, there was a strong message that the service provided – and the people providing that service – would be the crucial differentiator'.

Young people, like other workers, expect to be given a realistic wage, fair conditions and the kind of job that offers potential opportunities for personal and skills development. They also look for an accreditation of the new skills they develop and to be able to put these skills into immediate practice in their workplace.

It is this concern for development and training opportunities that young people seem to value and it is these sorts of criteria that indicate to a potential employee whether a job is a 'dead end' one or not and given a choice, will determine the appeal of one employer over another.

In Table 2 from the Perception study undertaken by Springboard UK (2012), the survey explored the appeal of the sector amongst secondary school pupils as a career choice. The results are disappointing and indicate that much more needs to be done to build awareness and promote a more positive image to them.

Table 2 Appeal of the hospitality sector to young people

	UK	
	Number	%
Not appealing	663	44%
Not too appealing	362	24%
I would try it	331	22%
Quite appealing	107	7%
Very appealing	41	3%

Source: Springboard UK (2012)

Less than a third of pupils across the UK found the sector appealing, suggesting that there is still significant work to be done in increasing the sectors appeal to young people. However, the fact that one in five said they were willing to give it a try is encouraging.

Knowledge of the sector was limited, with more than two thirds saying that they knew nothing or very little about the industry. This suggests that there is scope to increase the sectors' appeal by promoting awareness of the range of career opportunities that the sector offers.

The hospitality industry has historically been blighted by a reputation of low pay, low status and long unsociable hours and in many ways this reputation is still deserving of some businesses. This reputation has largely come about 'through connotations of servitude and inferiority' (Ehrenreich, 2001) and that these 'inferior workers' are encouraged to adjust themselves to the style and preferences of their customers (Leidner 1993, p.171). Basically, it is being argued that the reputation is one of a dead end job that 'inferior people' just have to put up with and act accordingly.

But with the rise of demand for hospitality things are changing and a new 'business of hospitality' has emerged, changing the status of its workers. Savvy employers are able to give their employees many more opportunities and career progression paths than was available previously. In grasping some understanding of what has changed it is easier to identify where old ways of doing things and attitudes in the hospitality industry have come from and also why they now need to change, for the sector to grow and flourish and to give equal opportunities to all young people seeking work. The industry urgently needs to address the skills gaps and create a pipeline of young people who will consider this industry as a career for the future and be prepared to commit to it. The question is where these young people will come from?

Current Study Findings

The following findings are based on a series of interviews and focus groups with representatives from the following stakeholder groups: hotel employers; young hotel employees; students studying hospitality courses at college; guidance teachers in a school and a college; and government sector skills managers responsible for hospitality and tourism.

In the research interviews, it emerged strongly that the different perceptions that stakeholders had of each other was inconsistent and in some discussions, founded on quite outdated views. This is not surprising with the fast pace of change, both within the industry and also within society culture – there are many factors that might lead this to be so. However these perceptions, however arrived at, are of crucial importance in shaping the expectations of both employer and employee.

Those working in the sector who were older, all agreed that hospitality had changed since their days of starting out and that the expectations put upon them then were very different to what they are today. In particular it was noted how the sorts of strict, often unreasonable and hierarchical behaviour of management and department heads has, in the main, disappeared. In addition, it was noted that recruitment in the industry had been very stable since 2008 because of the huge influx of migrant workers, who filled many of the industry's vacancies. These mostly Eastern European migrant workers were in their early to mid-20's, and were presentable and very keen to work. So it was easy to find an experienced, personable and smart young person for a low salary.

However as the European economy has started to recover, many of these migrant workers have moved on and the healthier economy encourages more mobility amongst all workers. Concern was expressed that the relatively strong 'employers market' will not be there forever and they expect recruitment to become even more challenging in the future. They also agreed that this will cause a shakeout in the industry which will expose who is a good employer with good practices and who isn't.

Having unfilled vacancies would seem to be a relative fact of life for many businesses with the main gaps being in the kitchen. This was endorsed by an employer who commented that at any one time they can have 'up to 50 vacancies out of a full staff of 850' and so recruitment is a continual concern.

Although this study has not focused in depth on the difference between the appeal of 'front of house' jobs versus 'back of house' ones, it is interesting to note the impact made by the media on the new respectability and appeal of cooking. This appeal is across the genders. However, from the findings in this study, it would appear that this impact is not yet making a huge impact on the pipeline of young people at school wanting to become qualified chefs in the kitchen: 'I thought it would be very strict in the kitchen and everyone with big tall hats – but it is not like that. You can speak to the other chefs without feeling you are doing something wrong. There is a good atmosphere there. Not Gordon Ramsey at all! It was much better than I thought it would be'.

Many of the young respondents agreed that a job in hospitality was not what they had thought it would be. For those school and college leavers starting their first job, there was a surprise at how fast paced and hard work it was. Several respondents spoke of colleagues having difficulties in keeping up and losing motivation because of it. These respondents commented that schools and colleges were out of date and didn't portray the industry as it really was. Another misconception that seems to be prevalent in the young college leaver is that the possession of a qualification would allow them to escape an entry level job and go straight into a supervisory or management position: 'Kids are coming out of school thinking they own the world – very few have a service ethic. They don't understand why they should mop up someone's drink when they throw it on the floor – that is where the Polish excel – they know that they need to serve to get on'(teacher).

A common complaint was that young people today have too much freedom and neither their parents nor schools challenge them enough. They discussed a sense amongst their peer group of not having to work hard for anything because parents or schools would just give rewards anyway so they didn't need to try.

Those respondents who currently work in the industry endorsed the industry for its positive experience 'Life in hospitality is a really fun job – the world becomes your market place – it is really FUN – and is a profession not just a job to make ends meet'. Whereas those who have limited or no direct experience tended to have an inaccurate idea of what jobs were available in hospitality. A common perception is that the industry has only the following four jobs; chef, cleaner, reception person, bar person. For this reason this industry is not commonly thought to have any advanced career possibilities, whereas in fact there are a vast number of jobs and many different career routes.

The industry too, has not helped this perception as some in management still hold on to the notion that one cannot work in management in hospitality unless you have had significant experience in food and drink operations. The employers stated that they would tend to look for attitude and then opt to train for the skills that they needed.

Even for more technically skilled job vacancies such as in the kitchen, there still would be a significant emphasis placed on soft skills such as appearance, time keeping, team working and a fit to company values. Schools reported that they teach softer skills in PSE classes (Personal and Social Education) but as there is no assessment on this subject, less focus is placed on it. However the question remains that if these skills are not instilled in a person by their families, and it is not a top priority for schools – who is it who then ensures that every young person is equipped with them?

A further challenge is observed with young people's appearance and the current fashion for expressing oneself through piercings and tattoos. This has become a big issue for employers who in part have somewhat relented on the subject, 'it is ok as long as they aren't seen'. Although one of the young respondents commented:

'People express themselves through tattoos – it says who you are. I have also got a tongue, nose and belly piercings done – I don't think it will stop me getting a job – for instance in Solid Rock Cafe – I could get a job there no problem with tats and piercings.'

The college respondent expressed concern about the lack of value that employers are increasingly placing on qualifications and their preference for in-house training. In his view this is unnecessary as the college provides this training. This duplication can only serve to confuse and so more clarity is required on the necessary skills required by employers for their entry level jobs. 'We teach them the correct way but when employers cut corners during work placement we have confused students'

However employers felt that some of the hospitality practices taught in the college were outdated with the industry developing at such a rate. A solution that was offered is that all lecturers be required to do a certain amount of practical work in the industry to keep their skills and teaching content relevant. One employer made the point about social media and how essential it is for all new recruits to be able to answer a customer complaint on Twitter or TripAdvisor appropriately. It was questioned whether colleges taught this sort of contemporary skill?

Career talks and recruitment fairs are another area of contention. Schools are regularly invited to recruitment fairs showcasing many employers, but it is rare that any hospitality professionals attend. A similar story emerges when businesses are invited to give a careers talk in schools or to help with work placements by the school.

Conclusions

Overall, the low awareness of the hospitality sector must be addressed and the focus placed on 'the business of hospitality' rather than projecting the lower aspirations associated with the term 'hospitality industry.' A far greater involvement by businesses is required in schools and colleges and this should involve a programme of business mentoring/secondments by young hospitality employees to provide support, career vision, motivation and encouragement to young people. Similarly, schools and colleges must prioritise a greater engagement with the hospitality sector to ensure their teaching practices are current and the individuals involved are not entrenched in old views and ways of working. To support this, there needs to be a greater emphasis and priority on teaching soft skills, work readiness and employability in schools.

Social Media and Employee Recruitment

By Marcus-Milan Arandelovic

Area General Manager, Benelux, Hilton Worldwide

Marcus-Milan Arandelovic was born and raised in Germany. As a graduate of l'École Hôtelière de Lausanne in Switzerland, he started his international career with Hilton Hotels in 1994 in Hilton Brussels, Belgium. With more than 22 years of experience with Hilton Worldwide across Europe, Milan was appointed area general manager Hilton Benelux in 2012. Overlooking six hotels in the Netherlands (4) and Belgium (2), Milan is primarily engaged with rolling out the operational and commercial framework of the properties in the Benelux. One of his last major projects was the construction of the new Hilton Amsterdam Airport Schiphol, which opened in December 2015. Milan is passionate about his work and it is his ambition to guide and inspire team members, guests and owners alike. He strives to be inspirational in leadership and developed a broad range of skills and qualifications.

The overall aim of this chapter is to assess the influence and value of social media in the decision making process of job selection within the hospitality industry. We have entered an era where the global reach of technology has revolutionised the way we work, live and communicate affecting business and private aspects of our lives. The internet is now a global phenomenon with a penetration of 85% of the worlds' 7.1 billion population in 2014 now having access to it, with 25% of the total world population using social media and 75% of that online population using one or several social media networking sites (Curtis, 2013). The number of users for the different social networking sites is expected to further grow exponentially. Companies can profit from social networking sites as they can gain meaningful insights on trends, markets and personal details of potential employees. On the other hand, individuals can in turn quickly gain insight into a company's values and content and decide whether or not they wish to be associated with this enterprise. These developments have a direct impact on talent management, recruitment and selection with social media as a vehicle for this process.

Previous Research

Talent management is considered an essential part of a company's success; shareholder value cannot be the only measure for success of a companies' performance, the talent a company holds in the form of its team member's contribution, skills and potential has become a key to its success (Baum & Kokkranikal 2005; Lockwood 2006; Lawler III: 2008). According to Fishman (1998), in the new economy, competition is global, capital is abundant, ideas are developed quickly and cheaply, and people are willing to change jobs more often. In that kind of environment, all that matters is talent.

Building upon this means it is important how a company chooses to engage with potential talents and what image (employer branding) it portrays. Common platforms used by companies to transmit an employer brand image are Facebook and Twitter.

Bratton and Gold (2003) state that recruitment has two critical issues, one being to attract people, but secondly and more importantly to attract the right people – companies need to define who they require and their expectations of these individuals.

Beynon et al., (2002) emphasize that it could potentially be challenging to only hire the best people as they might be overqualified and hence the position may not live up to their expectations and they may leave. The opposite would mean having a shortage of people considered the best and as a result the organization would not be able to compete in a global marketplace with a less than capable workforce.

A recruitment process should therefore be seen as a dynamic process where the employee as well as the organisation experience whether or not their interests are complementary. A combination of attitude, skills, education, experience and abilities might be important to find the perfect fit for both, employer and the talented individual.

In recent years, recruitment has taken advantage of technology and e-recruitment has evolved as a means to reach out to candidates. E-recruitment and recruitment via Social Networking Sites (SNS) should not be seen as a replacement to traditional recruitment methods; however it should be viewed as taking recruitment to another dimension in finding the best match between a candidate and the organisation (Jones et al., (2002). The shift from manual to electronic recruitment has several advantages; some of which are listed below (Jones et al., 2002; Lee, 2005; Singh & Finn, 2003):

- Less costly
- Less resource allocation
- Global reach rather than only local reach (multi-language reach, global penetration)
- Time efficiency (vacancies are available for shorter periods of time)
- Competitive advantage versus competition

- Better employer branding as company is perceived as modern and up-to-date
- Personalized approach

Perry and Tyson (2008) describe however that it is not enough to change to online recruitment; a company needs to undergo a more strategic change of their recruitment process as a whole. Since the advent of the internet and the world wide explosion of social media usage, businesses feel the pressure to engage where their potential talents' activities are taking place – this is increasingly virtual on social media platforms. Nowadays, organisations need to anticipate what their different stakeholder groups want, and what their expectations and needs are. Duffy (2010) suggests that a company's website is no longer the main source of information. Social media allows people a voice in the business before they choose to work for a company and this voice can be heard globally (Sison 2009). In today's world, it seems that social media recruitment is standard for recruiters; in a recent survey amongst 1855 recruiting and human resource professionals, 93% state they use social media at one stage of the recruitment process (Jobvite 2014). Tang, Gu and Whinston (2012) point out that the benefits of engaging in social media have evolved from simply social sharing to employer brand building and recruitment. A recent study by Jobvite (2014) on how social media is used for recruiting has revealed that LinkedIn continues to be the most popular tool, with 94% of recruiters currently using it. Facebook comes second with 66% and Twitter third with 54%.

Research suggests that social media appeals to a younger audience. For example, a recent survey conducted by OnePoll and sales company software Salesforce found that 76% of university graduates would be attracted more towards a company that has a strong online employer brand and is actively using social media (cited in IDS 2013). Other research suggests that generational differences can influence who is likely to be attracted by social media recruiting, e.g. Generation 'Y' could be less concerned with privacy as older generations (Peluchette and Karl, 2009). With this in mind, companies would need to clearly define what profile they wish to have for a position in order to choose the right platform.

Notwithstanding the discussion above it is important to note that social media cannot be seen as a solution to all recruitment challenges of the industry, but as a tool to engage in a unique way with candidates through the opportunity for two-way dialogue and scalability (Mayfield, 2008). It is important to realize that in order to successfully recruit on social media, a company needs to elevate from a generic knowledge of how the various sites work to defining a clear online recruitment strategy. This however seems to be a challenge, as a study by Jobvite (2014) reveals, while 94% of all recruiters use LinkedIn for recruitment, only 18% claimed to have expertise in social recruiting.

According to Stoller (2012), organizations that have mastered social media information tools are seeing numerous advantages which involve an active dialogue with key stakeholder groups, clients and employees. When used properly, social media can enhance nearly all aspects of recruiting.

Current Study Findings

These findings are based on a questionnaire sent to students of the three major hotel management schools in the Netherlands, employees of a hotel chain in the Netherlands and interviews undertaken with executives of hotel companies and a social media expert.

The hotel executives underlined the importance of classifying recruitment as a corporate responsibility and making it part of a company's broader story. He emphasized that neither recruitment and selection nor social media nor any other aspect of a hotel company should be seen singularly or 'as a silo', bur rather in a combined context of employer branding and brand building. One of the more noticeable differences was that they identified the current workforce as ideal ambassadors to tell a company's story.

The findings from the student questionnaire also revealed that 85% of all respondents follow a brand or a company on social media which clearly shows the importance for companies to not only be present on social media but to also have a defined strategy about their social media presence. Furthermore, 56% of all of the students actively seek job opportunities via social media.

Respondents were asked about their preferred social media channel used to search and inform themselves about a potential employer. Unanimously for both, students and employees, this was via LinkedIn, followed by Facebook and Twitter, although almost twice as many preferred LinkedIn over Facebook in both the student and employee groups. This is despite the fact that many of them spend four times more time per day on Facebook.

This could be seen as an opportunity for companies to link e-recruitment tools to their Facebook and LinkedIn profiles to further increase their brand penetration. All interview responses and the questionnaires clearly demonstrate that social media is used by companies as well as students and employees.

Social media is all about engagement and hence needs to be managed and monitored closely. Research suggests that this can only be done if this is done by a specialist.

Furthermore, the executive respondents pointed out that it is important to have a unified message throughout all media. Social media should be part of a company's overall strategy and reflect the values and story of the company.

The answers from the questionnaires indicate that the preferred content or information on social media should include job opportunities, hotel openings, brand developments, new innovations, hotel news and special offers.

The findings show that there is an opportunity in becoming more proactive as an industry, and embrace the fact that the image of the hospitality industry needs to be changed as a whole to make an impact. Social Media can play an important role to do so, yet coming back on Brouwer's point this can only work if it becomes a strategic choice.

An important aspect to take into consideration is the long term success of any channel or platform. Consequently, social media should be considered a vehicle and the more generic topic of online content marketing should be seen as a business solution. A company needs to understand that employer branding and storytelling are the aspects to focus on at first, before deciding on the channel to communicate them with the public. These platforms can change fast, and the research suggests that a popular social networking site such as Facebook is not necessarily the best recruitment tool, however, if it is linked to employer branding communication, it can generate the highest positive reach.

Based on the data collected, the findings show that talent management, recruitment and social media are closely connected. At this point in time, both employers and potential employees frequently use social media in many aspects of the business, and not just as a source of information or initial screening. The different platforms can generate the right exposure to get 'liked' by the users and grow a company's reputation and reach as well as enhance the employer brand.

The online branding and presence of a company has a strong influence on users of the various social media sites; e.g. companies with more likes on Facebook will get more social validation and generate more posts, comments and hence awareness amongst users. Done by specialists, this should lead to greater corporate enthusiasm and consequently positive brand perceptions for any company and have a direct influence on the people wanting to be associated with this company and ultimately be employed by them.

Finally, the results reveal that through the triangulation of talent management, recruitment and selection, social media and building upon the employer branding communication and choice of platforms, there is a distinct influence of this online content marketing on a persons' job decision making process. A further conclusion is that none of the above aspects can be considered singularly but need to be embedded in a company's global strategy to achieve the desired corporate enthusiasm.

Developing an Innovative Corporate Culture

●

By Joanne Taylor-Stagg

Divisional Director, ReDefineBDL

Joanne Taylor-Stagg is currently the Divisional Director for ReDefineBDL. Before her appointment as such, she was General Manager of The Trafalgar Hotel in Central London commissioned with positioning and re-launching the property in the luxury lifestyle market as the hotel is undergoing a full refurbishment.

She started her career at The Carlton Hotel, a 5-star property in South Africa as a Management Trainee thereafter joining The Balalaika Hotel & Crown Court as Assistant Banqueting Manager. In 1995 she moved to the UK and was recruited as Food & Beverage Manager at a hotel in Wiltshire before joining the Marriott Group progressing quickly from Restaurant & Bar Manager to Food & Beverage Services Manager, Director of Operations and General Manager in 2006. Joanne's desire to lead a London Hotel through the Olympics brought her to the Crowne Plaza London Docklands, winning Hotel of the Year in 2012 and 2013. In 2014 she was appointed as Cluster General Manger before taking on the role of Divisional Director for ReDefineBDL. Joanne is a Member of the Royal Academy of Culinary Arts, a Member of the Institute of Hospitality and Chair of St Julian Scholars.

In an industry that so heavily relies on people, creating an innovative corporate culture in which the way things are done is in keeping with your ethos, is critical. This chapter defines what is required to develop and maintain an innovative culture.

Previous Research

In this chapter organisational culture is defined as "the way things are done in an organisation based on a firmly held set of beliefs, assumptions and values". The main reason culture appears to impact on innovation is that it makes employees accept innovation as a part of the organisation, and becomes integral to the way the organisation operates. For this innovative culture to grow, it needs to be born from the company's values. The question, therefore, is: "What core values need to be in place to foster an innovation culture?"

In their 2013 study, Manohar and Pandit highlight how innovative organisations have similar cultural traits. The study paid particular attention to whether the organisations' core values and beliefs contributed to their consistent success. The authors discovered that not only does each of the organisations have a set of core values that contribute to its success, the same core values can be found in all innovative organisations, these are: intense customer focus, product quality, innovation leadership, striving to be a pioneer in the industry, and profits.

In their article "Managing for Creativity", Richard Florida and Jim Goodnight propose that for leaders to get the best work from their employees, leaders should remove distractions, keep the workforce intellectually engaged, and act as the catalyst for creativity. Encouraging customer interaction, and engaging employees to also become creative partners, helps deliver superior services and products; ultimately, creativity and innovation are the result of interactions and relationships between all stakeholders.

The most innovative organisations have found a way to harness the creativity and inventiveness of the whole organisation. Brian Leavy (2005) argues in "A Leader's Guide to Creating an Innovative Culture" that finding and attracting talent with diverse skills, backgrounds, personalities, experience and from various industries can be a catalyst for innovation. Having the ability to recruit that talent becomes critical in finding innovators with the right fit for your organisation. Consideration also has to be given to ensuring that the correct balance between innovation and efficiency is achieved, with the ability to turn creative thought into commercially viable opportunities.

The challenge lies not only in setting up a creative culture but in the need to constantly evolve and develop it, in line with the changing dynamic in which the organisation operates. A recent case study conducted by Ghazzawi, Metinelli-Lee, Palladini and Hills (2014) "Cirque du Soleil: An Innovative Culture of Entertainment" demonstrates the elements required of an innovative culture in an organisation built on entertainment. Cirque du Soleil relies on live performances and it is the audience's perception of performance that defines the company rather than having a tangible product, as in manufacturing. Cirque du Soleil has remained one of the most successful entertainment companies, with its unique blend of circus acts, acrobatic stunts and dance performance. Cirque du Soleil's founder, Guy Laliberté, believes the company's culture and values provide a deep emotional connection and although never posted on a wall, they should reach everyone in the organisation through the way the team acts, works together and how they conduct themselves. The company culture relies on an ability to overcome artistic and cultural differences, especially as the performers generally live in close quarters. Strong communication and ethics build trust and create a community or family among the employees. From the outset, Laliberté encourages his employees to be open and accepting of people and encourages them to explore different ways to do things. He was insistent that "No is not a word… and impossible is not a word at Cirque du Soleil". Each performer must be happy to benefit the whole performance; the team and family is more important than the individuals therein. To foster a sense of family and connectedness from the outset, recruits – especially those from remote locations or when there have been dire home circumstances – are encouraged to bring two friends or family members with them when they join Cirque du Soleil. This helps them to quickly settle in an environment that will initially be foreign and challenging. The performers, and their children, receive education and language courses. The troupe also has regular parties to celebrate diversity. By putting the performers' happiness at the forefront of the company's philosophy, Cirque du Soleil maintains that the audience experience a more emotionally-driven, unique and extravagant performance.

In a case study of General Electric (Barlett and Wozny 2005), Jack Welch is quoted as saying "A company can boost productivity by restructuring, removing bureaucracy and downsizing but it cannot sustain high innovativeness without cultural change". Throughout his tenure as CEO, Welch kept reinforcing the company culture through various initiatives. In 1989 he focused on creating a culture based on candour, honesty and facing reality. He wanted everyone to feel heard and to be engaged. In 2000, he concentrated on how GE would be "a place where people have freedom to be creative, a place that brings out the best in everybody. An open, fair place where people have a sense that what they do matters, and where that sense of accomplishment is rewarded in the pocketbook and the soul. That will be our report card."

Overall the literature suggests that company values are essential in setting the tone of the corporate culture, where and how the company focuses its priorities, and are critical in establishing a successful innovative culture.

Current Study Findings

The current study involved four group discussions with personnel in a cross section of individual hotels within a medium size hotel management company. The discussions included the Executive Committee, Functional Heads of Department from the support areas of the business; Divisional Directors who oversee groups of hotels representing Operations; and Hotel General Managers.

One of the interviewees articulately summed up culture as: "A constant thread woven through everything we do and say". To develop that thread, the biggest challenge an organisation faces in stimulating innovation is in defining its mission well enough that people in the organisation understand it but not so much that it stifles creativity. Whilst people accept the mission, it should be adaptable to each business unit and team. Team members also wanted more examples of what the mission looks like in practice. One way of achieving this would be by sharing instances of the mission as not only a way of defining it, but also as a means of inspiration for those who may not be as creative or confident at sharing their ideas. These good examples should be frequently highlighted throughout the business using varying forms of communication from Facebook posts, to revamping and using the intranet, and creating a "mission related award" at the annual awards ceremony.

Values

An organisation's values need to be communicated both by subtly incorporating them into regular communication but also by making them visible in "back of house" areas. An effective way to make the values more visible in the business would be to ensure the leadership is demonstrating these values in a sustained and repetitive way. The leaders could publically commit to an action within a cyclical timeframe to drive the mission by linking it back to a value or values. There was also a view from the research that people are often "too polite" to one another with not enough challenge in the company, the values could provide a framework in which to increase this challenge without making it feel personal.

For the values to continue being the guiding light in the business, every effort must be made to recruit individuals with similar values to that of the company. The opposing but equally important requirement is to remove people who do not demonstrate the values, no matter how good their results are.

Trust

There is often a need to build trust between the leaders, support functions and the hotels and provide more opportunity for teams to work together. This may involve using technology such as the new "Office 365" meetings facility to host virtual meetings between the offices. Alternatively, it may be possible to set up quarterly "speed dating sessions" where the support functions and hotels mutually agree priorities. In addition, a review of goals needs to be undertaken, ensuring all employees receive not only their individual and departmental objectives but also cross-functional ones that enhance teamwork. Rewards need to be tied to these goals and could even be enhanced for initiatives that are rolled out across multiple business units. Another method is increasing the focus on performance, not just results. This will ensure recognition of an organisation's best performers despite market conditions that are beyond the individual's control. These interactions, unified approach and cross-functional objectives should combine to create better teamwork and trust. The new levels of trust should further aid the ability to challenge one another in more constructive ways.

Processes and Reporting

The resounding feedback from the participants in terms of processes was to avoid creating too many processes but instead to limit them to what is necessary, and especially, the statutory ones. Any new process should be interrogated to determine if it is necessary, and whether it solves the issue it is designed for. If not, then the root cause should be addressed instead. There will be situations in a company where change is the norm and processes may have to be implemented to temporarily address a different issue; so when this is the case, it should be acknowledged as such and a timeframe established to review its on-going necessity.

Reporting could be enhanced by adapting a strategy similar to that adopted by GE, "Real Time Planning", in which a "play book" is done for each business. The book would set out: current market dynamics, the competitors' key recent activities, the greatest competitive threat over the next three years, and the organisation's planned business response. This would provide the hotel owner with a succinct yet clear plan for his or her business and tie the management company into its longer-term success.

In order to reduce bureaucracy and get parties to work out new ways to tackle existing challenges or innovations, a leader should present a challenge to the team, with a broad agenda; the employees are then allowed to work on this alone, or with the aid of a facilitator. The suggested solutions are then proposed to the leader, in the presence of his or her boss. The leader must then make an instant decision on the proposals by agreeing to implement them, or refusing to do so while giving reasons, or by asking for more data to be provided by an agreed future date.

Recruiting and Managing Talent

To find new innovative talent, networking beyond the obvious areas needs to be encouraged, for example, by attending events beyond the hospitality industry where people with compatible skills meet, e.g. finance people. Opportunities should also be sought, and taken, to speak at hospitality industry events to raise the profile of the management company. In terms of identifying and developing younger talent, "reverse mentoring" could be used. This means each leader in the business identifies an area they want to explore further, for instance social media, and a younger member of the company, ideally in another function or hotel, could act as a mentor to the leadership. This would detect talent throughout the business and also enhance cross-functional working. This would naturally sit alongside the mentoring that already takes place in a business, but could also enhance it.

The issue of consistent benefits needs to be addressed and solutions explored wherein hotel staff members, particularly GMs, can move between hotels and retain their benefits regardless of hotel ownership. A possible solution would be for a management company to employ the hotel GMs directly, and recharge their remuneration package to the hotels instead of it being a direct expense. A limitation will be how to ensure that even with the natural flux of hotels, the GMs can still be contracted to the hotel so that if a hotel should leave a management company, the GM still has a job.

Resources

In terms of resources, whilst it was largely agreed that funding for innovation should not come from a shared pot, there is a need to improve the way management companies and the hotels request additional funding from the hotel owners. The asset team could provide training to the GMs on how to determine an appropriate level of return for each project and how to write a pitch document for the owner. For smaller innovations with less financial risk, there needs to be a consistent "fail fast, fail cheap" message sent to the hotels stating that a degree of overspend on budget will be accepted if there is the possibility of a realistic return.

The ability to create time to think was also universally recognised as a resource requirement to aid transformation. There needs to be a way to ring fence "thinking time" either for individuals or for groups. Whilst most respondents agreed this responsibility should fall to individuals themselves, this practice is not currently occurring and unless a change is made, it is unlikely to occur. The acceptance of "thinking time" also needs to be addressed as several participants felt the rest of the organisation would not be supportive of this time and sarcasm or banter would undermine it being adopted. The "work out" sessions mentioned above would provide a forum for this. Another solution would be to utilise a facilitator to assist the leadership to place more value on preparing for the future.

Performance Measurement

In conclusion, a company needs to be strong at capturing learning from both successes and failures and this should be viewed with the same importance as "thinking time" and could be addressed in a similar way. The view of success needs to be adapted to be more flexible. Whilst an agreed set of objectives should be shared with the hotel owners and form the basis for any remuneration, internal goals could also be reviewed quarterly to keep them relevant. Where a function or hotel is meeting its targets, these goals should be stretched to further enhance performance. Where these targets become unlikely, due to external factors, new goals could be set internally to motivate the team to keep striving towards stepped goals. Attention must be given to ensuring failure on stretched goals is not punished as it is more important to encourage ambition and get people to think in a transformational, as opposed to an incremental, way. Rewarding noble failures will reinforce this. As previously stated, there should be cross-functional as well as individual and departmental targets to ensure total corporate success.

Conclusion

The literature review raised a view that the organisational culture most likely to succeed at innovation is the adhocracy culture, where flexibility is coupled with an external focus. Management companies need to think seriously about developing an innovative culture and find ways to benchmark and learn from the best companies, regardless of industry.

Boutique and Lifestyle Brand Positioning

By Beverly Payne

Director Accelerate Hospitality

Beverly Payne is a hotelier by profession and by heart. She is currently the General Manager at the Conrad London St. James.

Her specific expertise lie in the areas of Hotels, Self-Catering and Exclusive Use Accommodation, Agritourism businesses, Spas and Golf as well as food and beverage related to the above.

She is equally comfortable with small and large operational challenges as much as large feasibilies and funding documents. The real joy is mixing both, working with very small businesses and large corporate groups. Beverly is committed to balancing consultancy and advisory roles with hands on leadership at the coal face whilst fulfilling interim roles at a senior level.

The hotel industry has seen significant change over the last ten years but particularly in the last five years where there has been a shift from more traditional brands to new brands that have been recently introduced, with the label either Boutique or Lifestyle Hotel. The hotel scene changed in 1978 when Anoushka Hempel opened Blake's in London, arguably the first Boutique hotel. In 1984 Ian Schrager's opening of Morgan's in New York led to the world's first Boutique Hotel group, a significant game changer leading to the phenomenon of 'Boutique Hotels'.

In 1998 Starwood Hotels opening of the W Hotel in New York was the first successful venture from a large hotel company to enter the Boutique market and at this point the tag 'Lifestyle' came into the hotelier's language. In 2005 IHG launched Indigo and claimed it as "the industry's first branded Boutique Hotel experience". In 2014 IHG acquired Kimpton Hotels the world's largest independent Boutique Hotel operator to create 'the world's leading hotel and Lifestyle hotel business' (IHG aquires Kimpton Hotel, 2014).

Currently the accommodation platform sees a myriad of new brands emerging as Lifestyle or Boutique. It is felt appropriate to challenge the labels and understand if the expectations of the customer are aligned with the owner's ambitions for their new brands.

The principle aim of chapter is to gain a better understanding of the positioning of hotels and hotel brands in the Boutique and Lifestyle segment, to ascertain what the consumer expects and understands of Boutique Hotels, what they are prepared to pay for, the current motivations of large hotel companies to enter the market with new brands and to explore how they plan to integrate them into their existing portfolios.

Previous Research

There is a lack of definition with the word 'boutique' at a general level. According to the English Dictionary, the word boutique is French in origin and describes 'a small shop or a small specialty department within a larger store, especially one that sells fashionable clothes and accessories or a special selection of other merchandise', and also as 'any small, exclusive business offering customized service'. It has since evolved and within all areas of business, media agencies and consultancy, activities are now described as boutique (Dictionary Reference, 2014). Boutique Hotels were developed by entrepreneurs outside of the sector who saw the opportunity to create an alternative style of hotel which would look and behave differently and deliver premium financial performance as well as making solid property development decisions.

There is also no real definition of lifestyle and this is further complicated as consumers often enjoy more than one lifestyle simultaneously which is referred to as fragmentation (Firat, 1991) . An example of this, in hotel terms, is a consumer may use a Premier Inn for business, but for leisure chose a Boutique Hotel. Consuming the service within a hotel may temporarily fill a gap in the consumers' aspirations to live another lifestyle and also can provide a crutch and mitigate risk when changing lifestyles.

The issue is consumers can readily turn off one lifestyle and make substitutions easily. This view is supported by (Aaker, 1997), who argues that consumers use brands to express and validate their self-identity and this self-expression can be linked to the notion of conspicuous consumption, a term used to describe the acquisition of products or services for the purpose of attaining or maintaining social status.

Adner acknowledges that the formal definition of the Boutique or Lifestyle concept remains elusive, but believes there is some agreement on a thematic, architectural style, offering warmth, personalised service and a relatively small number of rooms aimed at a target market of 20 – 55 year olds (Adner, 2014).

Traditionally the hotel market was segmented by scale (level of luxury) location, type of customer (business and leisure). Large hotels were run with strict brand standards that led to a rather 'commodity' approach with efficient but perhaps rather impersonal service. The larger players when Boutique Hotels were emerging were focusing on segmenting the market further by offering a range of hotels with different levels of brand standard.

Factors that accelerated the acceptance and demand for Boutique Hotels was access to the GDS via travel websites, development of more and affordable airline routes, the increase in disposable income and the desire for personal service.

Agreeing on a definition appears now to be of urgent focus within the sector as Boutique Hotels seek differentiation from the larger chains that are entering their space. Descriptions continue using the same old buzz words and vocabulary for example, culture, design, individual, unique, urban, personalised, creative, location based. Boutique Hotels are often older in historical buildings, and Lifestyle Hotels tend to be more contemporary (Wolff, 2008)

The BLLA commissioned research in 2012, (Day, Quadri, & Jones, 2012) to ascertain which words most defined Boutique and Lifestyle Hotels. Based on the research Boutique Hotels 'are typically small hotels that offer high levels of service, Boutique Hotels often provide authentic cultural or historic experiences and interesting services to guests, Boutique Hotels are unique'. Lifestyle Hotels 'tend to be small to medium sized hotels that provide innovative features and service. They tend to have contemporary design features .They provide highly personalised service that differentiates them from larger hotels brands'. (Day, Quadri, & Jones, 2012)

Current Study Findings

The research involved a programme of nine in depth interviews with representatives of operators in the boutique and lifestyle hotel sectors and three group discussions consisting of 25 hotel consumers. The key findings were as follows:

Definitions and understanding of Boutique and Lifestyle Hotels

In the main Boutique Hotels were thought to be luxury, however, subsets of boutique were generally accepted as being feasible across other accommodation platforms. Overall Lifestyle Hotels are currently seen as a subset of boutique; larger hotels with some aspects of boutique integrated, all rooms being the same with more sophisticated technology.

What is of particular concern is the industry itself does not particularly like the term 'lifestyle' or agree on what it is, which readily explains why the customer is confused. What is contradictory is that most of the new brands created are classified as Lifestyle Hotels, but the industry claims it does not fully understand what they are. Lifestyle, all agree is 'trending'. Indigo as a brand has caused some confusion, whilst claimed by IGH as the world's largest boutique hotel brand; all three focus groups identified it visually as a Lifestyle Hotel. Newly refurbished traditional brands were also identified as lifestyle. Marketing teams possibly need to focus less on defining what a Lifestyle Hotel is and more specifically focus on what 'lifestyle customer' each brand is appealing to.

With consumers, the label Boutique Hotel definitely means something; however, the label Lifestyle Hotel does not. Boutique hotels are still mainly used for leisure stays. The research concurred with the literature on the importance of female buying power in purchasing and most interestingly, how they select hotels is quite different to males. Females tend to spend much more time online searching for hotels, reading lots of reviews and looking at web sites and press 'hot lists' whereas males make the choice more speedily and were much more likely to use their loyalty card for business and short stays. Loyalty cards overall were more relevant to the male decision making process for business than to their female counterparts. Females appear to hold stronger views that boutique hotels should be independently run, whereas males more readily accepted that global companies can operate a number of different brands successfully in many different markets.

Location is usually the start point for selecting a Boutique Hotel and customers let the location dictate the facilities required in the hotel. Restaurant facilities are not important unless it is a destination restaurant, however, the bar and communal spaces are important. In Lifestyle hotels there was an expectation of some leisure facilities.

As the sector expands into the business sector which is expected as the customer becomes more educated and the number of hotels in the sector increases this will have implications on how marketing teams position hotels to women and men differently. The larger companies expect their customers to move through their brands, but in order to do this the brands will have to have meaning and not just be a badge to avoid customer confusion.

Strategic decision to integrate new brands into portfolios

The decisions by the major hotel chains to enter this segment are for two main reasons; financial and a response to customer demand. Boutique Hotels have always outperformed the market but Starwood showed with W that the boutique model could be tweaked to a larger scale successfully. It's a model that works, has high appeal, builds are cheaper, there are no unnecessary facilities, and it is also flexible enough to work into existing buildings where traditional brands won't. Add to this higher room yield and lower payroll, but it was not really a boutique hotel so marketers positioned these hotels as 'Lifestyle' and everyone has followed the trend. They respond to the local destination and this drives the facilities on site, together with low interest rates, tax efficient investment schemes for using existing empty buildings has all accelerated the growth and made more projects viable.

These new brands almost go full circle back to the original boutique model, limited or minimum food in the corporate hotels and 'uber cool' food and beverage 'from the independents' with bars being important in both. For the global companies, this is an exciting new model as owners are looking for more profitable franchises with better returns and they can now do this on a smaller number of rooms.

The research highlighted the view that the new brands would not be integrated easily into the corporate companies and it's generally accepted that these brand teams would need to have a different skill set from traditional brand teams.

Future trends

In summary, the last ten years was seen as a period of profound shift in the hotel sector and the principal change has been the rapid increase in the new brands, which have principally been in the Boutique and Lifestyle segment. In the next ten years the marketplace for both Boutique and Lifestyle Hotels will more than likely be defined through education and experience as more customers actually stay in the new brands.

Until now the dominant market segment has been leisure, but as more bedrooms come to market in the Boutique and Lifestyle segment it's inevitable that the business segment will play a more significant role.

Many of the new brands are effectively 'fashion hotels' and the question has to be asked what happens with longevity on more fashionable Boutique Hotels when they fall out of fashion? There will always be bigger, better, newer and different coming soon, but as they don't want design to date, does this lead to less striking design at the outset?

It is predicted that many independent hotels and small groups will continue to be swallowed by large companies, this will have a profound effect over time on how these are also integrated, badged, repositioned but also the impact on the customer as the independent boutique operator disappears.

The expansion of new brands will impact on how existing stock is positioned and refurbished; differentiation has to be the key to avoid customer confusion. "The big hotel chains are in the business of pretending they aren't big chains. They want you to think they are Boutiques," says Pauline Frommer, editorial director for Frommer's, the travel guide company founded by her father, Arthur Frommer. "This dizzying array of brand names is a good way for them to hide. The vast majority of the public is not going to keep track." (Mayerowitz, 2015) However, if a Holiday Inn potentially looks like an Indigo which looks like a Park Place; one being a traditional brand, one claiming to be a Boutique and one a Lifestyle, how is the customer to understand and keep pace with this complex market place?

The Impact of Recession on Consumer Behaviour and Implications for the Hotel Industry in the UK and Ireland

●

By Craig Gardner

Regional General Manager, Hilton

Craig Gardner has gathered over 25 years' experience within the hospitality industry where he has successfully held a number of roles across Europe. Craig started his career in Edinburgh and has had the pleasure of working within the industry throughout the UK, Ireland and Sweden. He is currently working for Hilton International where he is the Regional General Manager for the Managed Hotels portfolio which covers the United Kingdom and Ireland. Craig recently graduated with distinction after successfully completing the Masters in Hospitality and Tourism Management at Strathclyde University.

The recent recession has been the most severe since the depression of the 1930s (Quelch and Jocz, 2009) and has had a great impact on consumer behaviour. Whereas previously the impact of recessions on consumer behaviour has been short-lived, it is suggested that the so-called Great Recession towards the end of the last decade has influenced consumer behaviour to a longer-lasting and larger degree.

The depth and longevity of the recession combined with factors such as the banking crisis and the extent of debt have led to changes in the way consumers perceive companies, brands and their own personal values. These changes have implications for businesses as they react to reductions in spending, changing consumer priorities and the emergence of new entrants into the marketplace who may be better suited to a new age of "frugality" (Piercy et al., 2010).

This chapter focusses on an area of research on which there is limited study, namely how these behavioural changes have influenced the hospitality industry in the UK and Ireland, an industry with a collective turnover of €163.8 billion (c.£120bn) and employing over 2 million people (Ernst & Young, 2013).

Previous Research

The recent economic crisis has been described as having a "severe impact on customer behaviour" (Hermann, 2009) and a profound impact on consumers and "will affect most markets and consumers in all economic strata" (Flatters and Wilmott, 2009). These changes have been called the new age of "frugality" (Piercy et al., 2010) (Hamm 2008) and the age of "thrift" (Gerzema and D'Antonio, 2010), the terms being reflective of consumer reactions in times of economic hardship to reduce expenditure by buying less expensive or non-essential items. Research has revealed that even before the recession there was mounting dissatisfaction with excessive consumption (Flatters and Wilmott, 2009) and that consumer thriftiness has been led by a reduction in "aspirational" shopping, as consumers suffered from "luxury shame" and felt guilty about buying indulgences" (Piercy et al., 2010). It is argued that this excessive consumption created the paradox of happiness, which states that once a basic satisfaction of want is achieved, happiness does not increase with acquisition or increases in income (Drakopoulos, 2008).

There is evidence that these changes may be long lasting. A recent research study showed that of those whose purchases moved from high-priced to low-priced products, "34% of the switchers said they no longer preferred higher-priced products" (Bohlen et al., 2009). The research also noted, "Normally, the premium priced product would return to favour as the economy bounced back, even if the willingness of the consumer to pay rebounds as the economy does, changes to the perceptions of the value of lower and higher priced may fundamentally alter what they choose to buy" (Bohlen et al., 2009). It is proposed with this in mind that consumers may not revert to the excesses of consumption and personal show of wealth displayed prior to recession. A recent study showed that "More than two-thirds of US respondents are moving toward a pared down lifestyle with fewer possessions and less emphasis on displays of wealth" (Gerzema and D'Antonio, 2010). It is also suggested that instead of seeking social status through the acquisition of goods, consumers are seeking satisfaction through a sense of "competency, self-sufficiency and accomplishment" (Gerzema and D'Antonio, 2010) and are seeking "more meaning, more connections, more satisfaction and more purpose" (Voinea and Filip, 2011).

This desire for a purchase more reflective of individual beliefs and values is moving away from gaining pleasure through acquisition and towards satisfaction gained from a more personal experiential exchange. It is also suggested that as "people are enjoying much more material comfort in comparison to previous generations" there is a resulting trend towards "personal fulfilment and aspiration through experience and authenticity" (Yeoman, 2011). It is also proposed that as economic downturns increase consumers' desire for simplicity in what is a stressful time, the growth of comparison sites to simplify choice has been aided, demand for trusted brands has grown, and the desire for "advisers" such as social media sites to assist in the simplification of consumer choice has increased.

Not only are consumers becoming more aware of the cost of comparative purchases across different brands but they are searching for discounts, which is becoming a more commonly attractive and more socially acceptable trend (Yeoman, 2011). It is argued that this willingness to compare on price is in part driven by the consumers' desire for simplicity, the availability of information through the Internet and in part by the number of brands available and the consumers' difficulty in differentiating between them: "The world is full of brands and consumers are having a hard time assessing the differences between them" (Gerzema and Lebar, 2009). Research has shown that there are drops in the key measures of brand value, such as awareness, trust, regard and admiration, that the overall perception of brands was eroding and that consumers trusted only 20% of brands, half the number of the previous decade (Gerzema and Lebar, 2009). This erosion of trust was also evident in business and civil society, which has been recorded by the Edelman Trust Barometer as markedly down in the period after recession (Beinhocker et al., 2009). Perhaps the greatest concern for highly recognised hotel brands is this erosion of trust, the definition of trust being "a feeling of security held by the consumer that the brand will meet his/her consumption expectations" (Delgado-Ballister and Munuera-Aleman, 2001). It therefore stands to reason that if consumers do not trust the promises brands make then loyalty to that brand, its value and the potential premium it may have in the market place diminishes. This may explain a further study which determined a large drop in consumer loyalty to brands in recent years; "40% of consumers showed a preference or commitment to one brand in a category in 2000 but that measure dropped to 10% by 2007" (Gerzema and Lebar, 2009).

Similarly, if branding is less effective because of lack of trust then there is less differentiation between brands in the eyes of the consumer, which allows for "commoditisation", i.e. customers looking at simpler methods of comparison, e.g. price and location may be dominating factors when comparing hotel accommodation.

Previously, consumers "downgraded" to low-cost providers during recessions and reverted back to their preferred brands as financial conditions improved. The "age of thrift" linked to the depth of recession when connected to deterioration in brand loyalty suggests that there is a greater possibility of profound transformations in consumers' attitudes and values (Quelch and Jocz, 2009) and that the "bounce back" may take much longer. In addition, as low-cost providers and budget brands also understand the value of consumer loyalty, they have been working hard to retain consumers by increasing their offering to compete directly with premium brands. Free Wi-Fi and improved bar and restaurant offerings at budget hotels such as Travelodge and Premier Inn and design-led budget hotels such as Citizen M have helped blur the lines and reduce the points of differentiation between budget and full-service hotels.

There has also been a disproportionate growth of hotels in the budget sector in recent years; (Whitebridge Hospitality Ltd, 2015) however, there are also other factors linked to the recession which provide compelling reasons for this growth, as detailed in a recent report. 1) Credit remains scarce and budget hotels typically cost less than €7.5 million for a 125 room model (excluding land cost); 2) Modular methods of construction reduce development time, and with limited public areas, smaller rooms and "no frills", developers have been able to make use of restrictive sites in terms of layout and size; 3) Catering to a transient market at the lower end of the price market, branded budget hotels can leverage their distribution through brand awareness to enter a market quickly; 4) Lower building costs, shorter development and market penetration time and the fact that financiers see a safer and faster return on investment mean that developers and operators are finding it easier to attract funding for budget hotels. 5) HVS (hotel valuation services) research estimates that in 2009 European branded midscale and upscale hotels dropped RevPar (revenue per available room) by 15-20% whilst branded budget hotels showed an overall decrease of between 5 and 10%. (Blanco et al., 2011)

Ease of financing in challenging economic conditions has played a part in this growth; however, similarly to the fact detailed earlier where low-cost providers were targeting "high-end" consumers who may have downgraded due to the economic downturn, budget hotels have introduced modern design, in-room technology and upgraded food and beverage offerings to widen their appeal.

Current Research Findings

Six research interviews were undertaken with experts, whose role in the hotel industry is concerned with the development, ownership and financing of properties and consumers who travel frequently and stay in hotels. In addition, two group discussions were also undertaken with hotel guests.

When reviewing the data collected from the primary research, it was clear that there was acceptance that there had been changes to consumer behaviour in the years since the last recession. The strongly held belief was that one of these changes was the seeking of "value for money" and "deals". There was also a belief amongst participants that consumers' usage of online information has made comparisons of hotels and greater understanding of products and pricing more prevalent, putting more thought into their purchases, partly driven by the "value for money" factor, and using the internet as a tool to assist them in being more discerning when purchasing.

It is argued that as a result of this behavioural change, hotel brands should ensure that their products are priced appropriately, discounting where appropriate, and that their value proposition is clear to the consumer. The quality of information available online which allows the consumer to make an informed purchase, along with the positioning of the hotel against competitors on third-party websites must also be viewed as a priority given increased transparency.

The reflection by participants that purchases associated with excess and "conspicuous consumption" were being replaced with more "experiential" purchasing which suggests that hotel chains should be communicating the benefits more than the features of their hotels using emotive language. The suggestion that the personalisation of a consumers' purchase would assist both in experiencing and in gaining more control is an area that should be developed further.

Consumer Attitudes towards Brands and Loyalty

Whilst conducting the primary research into attitudes towards consumer loyalty and trust in brands, it became clear that there had been a change in consumers' attitudes towards brand loyalty, partly driven by greater visibility of product and recommendations from other consumers. Industry experts also concurred with these views; however, they were more specific in their reasoning, a common theme being the identification of "best product in the location" aided by insight gained through comparison sites. This suggests that there is a clear move to "mercurial consumption", with customers flitting between brands based on their own and others experiences rather than brand or marketing promises. This is partly due to the ability to compare products and make decisions on information readily available online. In addition, there are clear links to the importance that the interviewees place on consistency. If the consumer does not know what to expect from a brand as a result of their experiences of inconsistency, then they will lose trust in the brand and this will impact on loyalty. In addition, the meeting of consumer expectations served as both a promoter of loyalty and as a potential area where loyalty could be influenced negatively. For regular travellers, loyalty programmes were also an important determinant of loyalty.

However, it stands to reason that the importance of online review sites and the reviews provided by consumers are of great importance, and hotels should strive to ensure that these reviews reflect positive reflections of consumer experience and positive differentiation from other products.

One measure of the impact of changes in consumer behaviour upon the hotel sector is reviewing the growth and development of hotel brands and sectors, as it is proposed that markets eventually reflect changes in demand driven by consumers. The interviewees indicated that the availability of funding to develop hotels was not just linked to the amount of funding available but to the perceived lower risk of budget properties in the marketplace. One of the key reasons for lower growth in the full-service sector highlighted was the cost of replacing or building of a new property compared to the cost of purchasing an existing property. In the current marketplace it is less costly to buy an existing property than to build a new one. It is argued that this has led to available funding being used to purchase distressed or unwanted assets rather than developing new ones. If property prices increase as demand becomes constrained, it is suggested that it may become more realistic to develop new full-service properties to increase volume growth in the sector.

Aside from the economic aspects which have led to greater growth in the budget sector, there was a clear view amongst participants that one of the defining factors was consumers' willingness to accept and pay for a more basic, no-frills offering, increasing the demand for budget accommodation. There was also data to suggest that the consumers' willingness to stay in budget hotels was linked to changing priorities where the hotel facilities and offering was viewed as less important than the experiential reason for visiting the location. Additionally, part of this growth had been due to the creation of a "new market" of consumers who cannot afford frequent hotel stays or of consumers who can only afford to stay in hotels on a more frequent basis because of lower pricing.

In summary, research into consumer behaviour concluded that there was evidence that consumers had changed their approach to purchasing, being influenced by intrinsic factors such as greater social acceptance of a "value for money" led approach where consumers seek "deals" and a move away from the acquisition of goods to more experiential purchases. Research which indicated consumers' desire for simplification and mercurial consumption leading to a drop in brand loyalty and the aforementioned focus on value are all highlighted as dominant or advancing trends. Extrinsic factors such as the economic crisis and the growth of online comparison sites were identified as promoters of this behaviour and linked to the secondary research notions of more "mindful consumption" and a desire for simplification.

When reviewing the attitudes of consumers to brand loyalty, research confirmed the suggestion that consumers were less loyal than previously thought and were more willing to switch to competitors aided by information available online. It is argued that hotels should ensure that its visibility on comparison sites such as TripAdvisor is given greater importance, and targeting of "positioning" based on consumer reviews should be a key priority.

Marketing Hotels to Generation Y

●

By Alok Dixit

Director of Operations, Marriott

Alok Dixit is the General Manager of Swansea Marriott hotel following senior management roles within Marriott, Intercontinental hotel group, Macdonald hotel group and Best Western hotels. Born and raised in India, he attended International Institute of Hotel Management in Kolkata graduating in 2000 with diploma in Hotel and Catering Management. Alok relocated to UK in late 2000 to pursue Bachelor of Arts in International Hospitality Management from Queen Margaret University. After over 11 years of operational experience in Hospitality Management, he enrolled for Master's Degree at Strathclyde University in 2013 and successfully completed Masters in Hospitality and Tourism Management in 2015.

Not every generation is alike nor should they be treated in the same way and it is apparent that the hospitality industry has consistently adapted to attract their target consumers. Emergence of Generation Y as the largest consumer group in the world combined with their distinct characteristics makes studying them increasingly important for the future of the industry. As a group, they are unlike any other generation; they are more numerous, more affluent, better educated and more ethnically diverse.

This chapter will focus on analysing current hotel actions to ascertain if the marketing and promotional efforts are in line with the Generation Y motivations for booking hotels.

Previous Research

Hershatter and Epstein (2010) state bluntly that Millennials are simply 'wired differently' than individuals from previous generations. Born between the advent of the Walkman and founding of Google, the members of Generation Y are unsurprisingly shaped by technology.

Their formative years occurred during a period of economic prosperity, which also included outsourcing, globalization and foreign investments. Some of the unique characteristics of millennials include: highly optimistic, idealistic, conventional, high expectation of self and goal driven. According to Sladek (2013) members of this generation tend to:

- Hate to be sold anything; instead they buy into products or services
- Have always been rewarded for participation and not achievement; this makes it difficult to motive them
- Don't seek to acquire stuff; this makes it difficult to pitch your product
- Can self-organise friends for grassroots activism and they trust their friends first and their parents second; this is evident from the success of online review sites impacting on buying behaviour
- Actively research prices before making purchases
- Are driven by a desire to make a difference and seek to do business with ethical, trustworthy organisations
- Expect exceptional service and value customisation
- Remain detached from institutions, but closely networked with friends. Loyalty is not a priority as they value friends and their own experiences more

Over the generations, technology has changed society in fundamental ways. Generation Y has grown up with technology and is used to having technology as a large part of their life. Generation Y's dependence on technology is evident and they tend to utilise social media to share their life experiences and stay connected with groups, friends and communities. Influenced by parents who value education and a work place that demands it, most Generation Ys recognise that key to their success lies in advanced education. This is evident from a record number of students going to colleges and universities. (Wey Smola and Sutton, 2002; Tulgan and Martin, 2001).

It has proved difficult to communicate with this generation of youth as research has found that they are individualistic, anti-corporate and resistant to advertising efforts (Belleau et al., 2007). They have high expectations of service quality and expect prompt and reliable service with visually appealing facilities and well-groomed staff (Kueh & Voon, 2007). Everything about them is around instant gratification, wow factor, the quality of personalised experience and integrity of company's core values. It is critical to understand this concept to tap into the potential of this generation as they already represent one third of all hotel guests.

Wright (2013) states, Generation Y attitudes are already driving hotel design, guest services, booking methods and marketing at a very rapid pace. In terms of design, newer guest room layouts include beds facing oversized windows, large & sleek TV's with one stop connectivity for guests' multiple electronic gadgetry. Lobbies turned into places to meet, relax and network alongside a range of self-serve options as well as hotel apps that sell in hotel services.

Although many alternative actions and activities are being adopted to support industry readiness to meet these Generation Y characteristics, limited research exists that analyses the success of these efforts and if they meet the needs of Generation Y guests.

Current Study Findings

A total of 4 semi structured interviews were carried out with industry leaders in the hospitality industry to provide a detailed overview of the actions taken by the sector to attract Generation Y customers. In addition, 50 Generation Y participants completed an online survey regarding their hotel purchasing behaviours.

The qualitative research identified that hotel companies perceive that they have a full understanding of inter-generation differences and that they have already implemented numerous actions based on their understanding of this cohort's motivations. The redefining of hotel facilities, layout and services provide evidence to support this claim. The industry is innovating and dedicating brands designed for this generation, examples stated were Moxy by Marriott, Canopy by Hilton and Element by Sheraton. They are also experiencing changes in hotel reservation methods, brand loyalty and communication. The hotel industry perceives that Generation Y travellers want three main elements: customized experiences, digital convenience and relevant information on social media. This was the recurring theme from all the qualitative participants and the hotels are implementing different actions and strategies to meet them. They are redefining their loyalty programmes and investing in them to adapt to this cohort and they are working to develop mobile booking apps with the aim of meeting future demand.

The findings from the Generation Y customer survey also identified that they opt for online reservation mediums compared to traditional telephone calls. They also rate free and fast Wi-Fi as critical. This was also registered as critical factor by the industry experts who all mentioned infrastructure upgrade to support this generation as demanding. The customers in this group rarely book hotels based on brand loyalty. However, brand loyalty was slightly more important among males and particularly middle income customers. It was also interesting to observe that the Generation Y participants ranked leisure activities (spa, shops and gym) in the hotel as a low impact factor for making the booking but industry experts continue to invest in these facilities.

Generation Y participants in the study rated online reviews and reputation as the most important factor motivating them to buy. Another aspect which supports the growth of online review is the trait of sharing and being involved in community. Overall the online medium is the best medium to communicate with them. One of the hotel chains stated that they had gone "Hollywood" by running their own studio to create short films, TV shows and webisodes that promote its various brands. Online views of each short film exceed 6 million views on YouTube. Other examples included effective management of online and TripAdvisor feedback.

In Hilton, apps that allow hotel guests to select rooms, check in digitally or order a burger before arrival are becoming standard mobile features, while social media like Hilton Suggests Twitter handle (@HiltonSuggests) shares recommendations from contributors around the world for everything from where to eat to what to do and see.

Overall it is evident that Generation Y motivations are based on three key factors; first is relevant information about the hotel on social media, second is digital convenience and third can be categorised as customized experiences based on individual needs. This cohort buying decision does not get massively impacted upon by brand loyalty and they tend to shop online for best deals suited to their requirements. This generation has tactfully announced its existence to the hotel industry and is already dictating changes to industry practices. There are some obvious barriers existing in the industry to implement change and they consist on funds, size of the company and time. But it is abundantly clear that change is required if the industry aims to continue attracting this cohort in future.

The Impact of Social Media Marketing on Hotel Success

By Thomas Healy

SVP Asset Management, Strategic Hotels and Resorts

Thomas G. Healy is executive vice president, asset management at Strategic Hotels & Resorts, Inc., where he has oversight responsibility for multiple brands, including Four Seasons, Ritz-Carlton, Fairmont, Marriott, InterContinental, Loews Hotels & Resorts, and Montage. He joined the company in 2006.

Healy has more than 20 years of hotel experience, primarily in development and hotel operations. Prior to joining Strategic Hotels, he served in development, property operations, sales and marketing roles for Starwood Hotels & Resorts. He has been the general manager for various properties where he received numerous awards for his contributions, including "Turnaround Hotel of the Year" for Westin Hotels & Resorts. Also, he was the opening general manager of the Sheraton Overland Park Hotel & Convention Center.

Healy is certified Six Sigma Green Belt and has held several roles on various non-profit boards and advisory boards, including the Overland Park Chamber of Commerce, Overland Park Convention and Visitors Bureau, Central New Jersey Boy Scouts of America, the chairman of Central Jersey March of Dimes Walk for the Cure, and Eden Institute Autism Services Works Board.

Social media is a popular marketing and communication platform used by hotels. However, many hoteliers are still searching to find the best way to demonstrate the impact of social media marketing efforts and the contribution to the hotel's bottom line. The primary objective of this chapter is to examine and provide hotel marketers

with a deeper understanding of how to evaluate social media ROI. Never before have companies had the opportunity to talk to millions of customers, send out messages, get fast feedback and experiment with offers at relatively low costs. And never before have millions of consumers had the ability to talk to each other, criticizing or recommending hotels without the knowledge or input from a company (Blanchard, 2011). As a result, social media has become an essential part of marketing and communications programs at individual hotel property level. As more and more hotels have embraced social media as a marketing tool, the attention on its effectiveness is rising and the inevitable question arises – what is the value? Many hotels are finding it challenging to measure the impact of social media and are still searching for the best practices and metrics so they can understand where to invest and target their social media activities. Without an evaluation, hotel executives cannot tell whether a social media plan is working or which factors are contributing to its success or failure.

Previous Research

Although some social media platforms such as Facebook have been around for almost a decade, it wasn't until recently that marketers started evaluating social media effects. Since there is no universally accepted measurement tool for social media; it has triggered much debate in the literature. In the past three years, several books have even emerged on this topic (i.e. Blanchard, 2011; Kelly, 2013; Macarthy, 2014; Powell, 2011). Literature suggests that there is no clear, effective method of measuring social media ROI and scholars disagree whether it can be done. Therefore, deep analysis of the argument in the literature is necessary to determine whether hotels can quantify the value of social media. The literature indicates that the majority of existing social media measurements are based on the "Return-on-Investment"(ROI) business model (Blanchard, 2011). In the popular article "ROI in Social Media" by Fisher (2009), the author examines the arguments for and against using the ROI metric to justify social media programs. Fisher states that most of the arguments against the measurement of ROI in social media revolve around the idea that "traditional ROI measurement is not adapted to social media, which focuses on people, not dollars"(Fisher, 2009). Similarly, Hoffman and Fodor (2010) argue that "turning the traditional ROI approach on its head is essential in measuring social media. They suggest that the focus should be on consumer motivations to use social media and measuring the investments that customers make as they engage with brands, as opposed to calculating returns in terms of customer response".

In order to understand the ROI from social media, Stelzner (2013) proposes that companies measure how much they spend on agency fees and social media marketing, and then compare it to the value of the conversions from social media. He recommends that companies should first set business objectives and then determine which set of tools with their corresponding metrics can best achieve them. Similarly, Blanchard (2011) encourages organizations not to settle for basic social media metrics such as followers and number of likes, but instead link back to organizational objectives. While his approach is grounded in an ROI method of measuring social media, he also highlights the value of non-financial outcomes, such as change in positive or negative mentions, a change in volume of impressions, an increase in video downloads, etc. (Blanchard, 2011).

Through Facebook, hotels can measure ROI by using traditional metrics that are part of the site. Those include metrics such as page views, unique visitors and TAT, which stands for talking about this that measure the activity on the site (Facebook, 2013). The growing demand of Facebook marketing has also stimulated companies to write software for their own site to measure ROI. For example, Adobe created an analytics programme, which it claims helps determine the monetary value of "likes" on the website (Wendlandt, 2012). Moreover, Wendlant (2012) mentions another scoring system called "Edgerank", which is an algorithm that determines what information appears on a user's newsfeed. He explains that the scoring system depends on "affinity (frequency of interaction between you and users), edge weight (number of comments, likes, and shares), and time decay (the age of the post)".

Etlinger et al., (2013), released a report titled "The Social Media ROI Cookbook, which describes a six-method approach for measuring social media ROI. The study collected "data from interviews with those in the social space as well as quantitative data from 71 brand and agency-side professionals on measurement experiences and practices" (Etlinger et al., 2013). Those six methods can be broken down into two categories: top-down and bottom-up. The top-down approach can be broken down into three different types of analysis: anecdotal, correlation, and single or multivariate A/B testing. The most common of the three top-down approaches is the anecdote analysis, which involves a verbal "share" of a relationship between a social media activity and a sale either through written or verbal communication. A correlation analysis measures the relationship between two items. It takes a certain type of social media behaviour (e.g. Facebook likes or Twitter mentions) and tries to establish a relationship between it and some other activity (e.g. revenue or number of rooms sold). The resulting value shows if changes in one item will result in changes in the other item. The study claims that this type of analysis is often used to establish a relationship between social strategies, tactics, and business outcomes. Multivariate and single A/B testing are methods of testing for a particular hypothesis and are most commonly used to test market perceptions. In this type of analysis the marketer attempts to understand the effectiveness of two versions of some type of content in order to determine which has the best response rate, for example compare metrics of customers that have been exposed to certain types of social media content to those who have not. Multivariate testing uses the same core mechanisms as A/B testing but compares a higher number of variables, and reveals more information about how these variables interact with one another. According to Etlinger et al., (2013), multivariate testing lets you compare alternative versions of the same page or element running simultaneously on your website by randomly assigning visitors to different groups, then comparing the data to see which version produces the best outcomes for your goal, for example increased conversion. This type of analysis has been widely used to understand how a particular advertisement, for example social media advertising, is resonating with your core audience. Like correlation analysis, multivariate and A/B testing provide strong insight into how social strategies and tactics affect business outcomes. It is also a widely accepted practice of measurement by digital marketing professionals and numbers of books have been dedicated solely to multivariate testing.

The three primary ways of tracking revenue impact using bottom-up techniques are: linking and tagging, integrated analysis, and direct commerce. The linking and tagging approach enables marketers to apply a short link, or cookie to a site in order to track the source of a conversion. The integrated measurement approach utilizes an application, typically installed on a social network (frequently on Facebook) in order to track the user's activity. The direct commerce method has the most potential for direct correlation to sales, for example creating a storefront on Facebook and selling guest rooms directly from there.

According to the report, each organization needs to consider its goals before picking an approach. The reality is that both types of approaches need to be utilized in some form to tell a complete story"(Etlinger et al., 2013). Furthermore, according to the study, the top-down methods are often the easiest to capture and they require the fewest number of internal resources. However, these methods are not very scalable and require the presence of an analyst with knowledge of tools and statistics. Whether a marketer is utilizing a top-down or bottom-up revenue tracking approach, the bottom line is that they need to be tracking ROI. The report also emphasises that marketers should be measuring the results of individual social media campaigns as opposed to a total social media marketing effort, as this provides an organization with more reliable results of their investments.

Current Study Findings

This study is based on three components. Firstly, the perceptions of 8 senior hotel executives in the USA were identified towards the ROI of hotel social media activity. Secondly, by data mining hotel reservation data to monitor the social media engagement of guests at a large branded Miami Hotel (fan base in excess of 20,000) prior to and post a reservation being made and finally, through an experiment running two targeted Facebook advertising campaigns at a) fans and their affiliates b) non fans

Senior Executives

All of the senior hotel executives intimated that they are struggling to measure the ROI of their total social media marketing effort. However, half of them reported that even though they can't measure their total social media marketing efforts, they are able to measure some ROI aspects of specific social marketing campaigns or channels. Some of the key performance measures that hotels use include: engagement rate (tweets sent, likes, comments, shares); number of fans; traffic to website; and guest comments that are derived from conversations that took place in a social media space. However, these measures do not fully measure the ROI. This has caused frustration in the industry, people claim that social media is effective but are unable to measure the effect. Half of the hotel executives interviewed (4 out of 8) did not have the necessary tools to track the customer from the attraction stage through to the conversion stage. Better measures would help managers adjust their channel specific marketing tactics, formulate online offers that attract top customers, better engage with customers online and improve the social media visitor-to-customer conversion rate. Many of the hotel executives mentioned that they also struggling with measuring social media ROI because of a lack of certainty around goals. The challenge is that social media goals frequently reflect the core functionality of the channel rather than the core needs of the business.

Engagement

In measuring engagement, the critical aspect was how to ensure that the data used was accurate. With so many reservations containing partial data, we had to ensure we had reliable matches in order to get to any conclusive answers. The reservations were scrubbed for email addresses, mobile phone numbers, first and last names and run through a 3rd party application programming interface called "FullContact" which was used to confirm with 95% certainty the matches between the interaction database and the reservation database. This method compared the email and mobile number and connected them to Twitter and Facebook accounts. We had three groups of reservations, the first were people with no social profile because the reservation data was bad or the individual did not have a social profile. The second group had a social profile but did not engage with the hotel and the last had a social profile and did interact with the hotel at least once over the period of time (pre-reservation through to departure). Based on the 38,244 reservations made during the period being investigated, only 1,996 (5%) could be identified as having a social profile. Of those 1,996, with a social profile, 512 (25%) of the reservations made engaged with the hotel at one point during their experience pre- reservation through to departure and most critically 12% of the 512 actually engaged with the hotel prior to making the reservation. What does this mean for the hotel community, 25% of the reservations who could be identified as having a social profile engaged with the hotel could be upsold a suite, marketed a reservation in the spa or restaurant and asked to return or had problem

Before or during their stay. These are impressive numbers and scream why you may need to engage with your customer on social media.

The Experiment

The experiment involved running two separate, highly targeted offers for two audiences: a) fans & their affiliated networks b) non fans. The offers were for a discounted stay on particular set dates if a booking was made within a certain time window. The results showed that Facebook Fans and their affiliated network are more likely to purchase than those users that are not connected to the hotel's Facebook page. Additionally, the results supported research showing that social media platforms help bring more traffic to a hotel website and increase bookings. In particular during the experiment: Facebook fans and their affiliated networks (friends and followers of the fans) are almost twice as likely to engage with offers advertised on Facebook; fans claimed 28% more offers than non-fans; fans and their affiliated networks showed a much higher engagement rate with the advertised offer content; fans click through rate for fans was 3 times higher than non-fans; fans also showed more of a propensity to share content with their networks; Facebook fans and their affiliated networks are more likely to convert into future guests, spend money at the hotel; twice as many fans and their affiliated networks as non-fans clicked through to the booking engine and made a reservation; in addition the offer distributed to Facebook fans generated 5 times the additional number of sales leads and conversions outside of the offer dates in comparison to non-fans.

The significance of this; while it might sound like common sense is people that follow you have a greater likelihood of purchasing from you, versus those don't follow you.

Overall, it is clear based on the data that fans have a greater propensity to purchase, share and engage when they are targeted by compelling marketing offers. The value of this information to the hotel industry is that there is a clear correlation between a "fan" liking you and that translating into a sale by either themselves or their followers. This increased propensity to buy is what and why you should focus on growing your fans and followers. Over time, as targeted marketing matures this will create a competitive advantage and assist with wining the market share from your competitors. This is a positive step, but there needs to be more evaluation and analysis on the topic.

Trends in Hotel Distribution

By Yousif Al-Wagga

Group Operations Director, Apex Hotels Ltd

Yousif Al Wagga studied Hospitality Management at Bournemouth University obtaining a BA (Hons) degree and a diploma from the Chartered Institute of Marketing. Prior to joining Apex hotels he worked in the London hotel market for a period of 10 years gaining extensive experience within chain hotels including IHG, QMH, Le Meridien, Thistle with his previous role being the General Manager of the Kingsway Hall hotel. In January 2005, Yousif joined Apex Hotels as General Manager to open the companies first hotel outside of London, the Apex City of London located in Tower Hill. This was followed by a further 2 hotel openings in London which led to him taking on the role of Group Operations Director and more recently Joint Managing Director with responsibility for hotel operations, sales, marketing and revenue.

Hotel companies have historically distributed their product through a number of channels. The evolution of the internet led to a plethora of new online intermediaries which were initially viewed by hotels as a useful way to shift unsold inventory. It is evident that hotels underestimated the change to consumers booking online, which allowed online travel agents (OTAs), such as Expedia to grow at a phenomenal rate. A number of issues have emerged as a result of these changes namely: increasing costs of distribution; channel conflict; shift to media consumption across multiple platforms in particular mobile and uncertainty around the efforts of the government to reduce the power of the dominant OTAs. The role of the hotel distribution manager has become an increasingly complex task in today's multi-channel environment. With limited research on this topic business critical decisions are often being made without a full appreciation of the likely outcomes. In order to gain a better understanding of the actions that can be taken to implement a successful distribution strategy, this project will follow a number

of steps to assess the factors that have influenced changes in distribution, identify the current distribution issues and discover practical recommendations in order to execute a successful distribution strategy.

Previous Research

The advent of the internet is probably the most significant change to impact hotel distribution in recent times (Buhalis & Law 2008). The OTAs were very quick to develop their technology and respond to consumer behaviour (Gazzoli et al., 2008). By reacting quickly and taking advantage of the hotels slow adoption of these changes OTAs grew at a phenomenal pace taking an increasing slice of the distribution mix. Between 2001 and 2010 OTA total room revenue share in the U.S. lodging market had increased from 1.4% to 7.7% (Smith Travel Research 2011). Another interesting statistic from this research was the total room night demand from OTAs was highest for independent hotels. A more recent online channel is the Meta Booking Engines (MBEs) which are websites that support the buying process with particular focus on price comparison (Runfola et al., 2012). MBEs trawl the internet aggregating the results from a number of OTAs and hotel websites (Kracht & Wang 2010). The MBEs are predicted to have an increasing influence on the booking process and compete for market share with the OTAs. Although MBEs have been around since 2005 when Sidestep was first launched (Sidestep, 2000, 2005) this channel has only recently been seen as a threat to the traditional OTAs shown by the acquisition of Kayak by Priceline in 2012 and Trivago by Expedia in the same year (Taylor 2012).

Adding further complexity to the online distribution mix is the increasing influence of so called "gatekeepers" (Google, Facebook, Apple) which have become the preferred points of entry for consumers shopping online (Green & Lomanno 2012). For example Google's move into the MBE arena with their Hotelfinder product present additional risks and opportunities for hotels. Similar to other MBEs Hotelfinder displays hotel pricing to consumers with data coming directly from OTAs and hotel websites. By clicking on the normally paid advert of the referring site, bookings can be completed on the specific travel website. (Green & Lomanno 2012) predict that this trend for paid referrals may take upwards of 50% of hotel business before being delivered to a hotel or brand and cost between 10% to 20% of revenue. The shift in power to search engines has also been highlighted by (Kracht & Wang 2010).

When a consumer does not have a particular URL or website in mind the consumer is more than likely to use a search engine. Consumers have certainly been quick to adapt from offline to online distribution. In the U.K. more than half of consumers book their holiday online and in Europe bookings made via online travel agents increased by almost 20% from 2010 to 2011 (YStats.com 2012).

With consumers making an average of 38 visits to travel sites before making a booking (Expedia Media Solutions, 2013) across a number of different platforms the importance of adopting an omni-approach to hotel distribution becomes increasingly important. Comparing the consumer experience offered by hotels versus that of an OTA across the various platforms it is easy to see why the likes of Expedia have become the favoured booking channel. Searches for hotels and destinations can be made very quickly as can making the final booking. Price transparency is another indirect consequence of the move to online intermediaries giving consumers further reasons to book and shop online. The OTAs and MBAs have undoubtedly contributed to a greater focus on price and this coupled with convenience is likely to be a major reason why these channels have gained an increasing share of online bookings.

The analysis of the actual cost of distribution by channel has received limited attention in the past with a dearth of information that details the optimal distribution channel mix for a hotel. In addition, advice on how to maximise the benefit of a particular channel is often incomplete. For example (Kracht & Wang 2010) advises travel industry players to ensure their websites are ranked high up on the search engine results by utilising pay per click (PPC) advertising. Bidding for key search terms can be very costly and lead to acquisition costs that exceed the commission expense if booked via an OTA. It is unlikely that independent hotels in particular will ever be able to compete with the likes of Priceline which spent $1.5 billion dollars in 2014 with Google alone (Schaal 2014). Understanding the true cost of distribution by each channel is a complicated task due to the different types of commission models and various marketing expenses related to acquiring bookings directly (Green 2013). Green advises hotels should understand the overall cost to acquire a customer broken down into how much does it cost to (1) attract the customer, (2) get the reservation and (3) get them to repeat this process for all subsequent visits.

To add further complexity to the distribution landscape there has been a shift in the past few years towards digital media consumption across multiple platforms. The adoption of smartphones and tablet devices has led to an almost doubling of time consumers spend on the core digital media platforms, desktop computers, smartphones and tablets between April 2007 to June 2013 (Comscore 2013).

As behaviour has shifted, mobile has become a more significant element in all relevant digital media markets, including video, search, advertising and commerce. In 2010 Google saw a 3,000% increase in hotel mobile searches compared to 2009 (Starkov 2011). Consumers are not only using their mobile device for searching but also to conduct transactions. In respect of hotel shopping, travellers are significantly more likely to shop via an OTA when using a smartphone (Phocuswright 2015). Several reasons have been given for the OTA advantage on mobile including their investment in technology creating a more user-friendly experience and the ability to aggregate hotel products across multiple suppliers affording travellers a broader view of options.

The development of the internet and adoption of multi-channel distribution has also increased the potential for conflict between hotels and their intermediaries. Both rely on each other but compete for the same customers using an array of tools to entice bookers such as best rate guarantees and rewards for booking direct. Any action taken by a hotel that favours customers to book direct is likely to be viewed negatively by an OTA. Price parity agreements and hotel positioning on their sites enables OTAs to yield significant control and influence over hotels a further cause of channel conflict.

A subject that has the potential to have a significant impact on established distribution intermediaries are the policies of national and local governments. The growing influence of OTAs has certainly caught the attention of the authorities throughout Europe. For example in 2012 the UK the Office of Fair Trading (OFT) launched an investigation in to the agreements made between Booking.com, Expedia and Intercontinental Hotels Group (IHG) and the potential unfair practices that were restricting each OTA's ability to offer discounts to consumers. The ruling that was made in January 2014 accepted formal commitments from the three parties that would enable OTAs and hotels to offer discounts on room rates to consumers that signed up to a membership scheme, and make one undiscounted booking with the OTA or hotel in question to be eligible for future discounts. Although this ruling was overturned in September 2015, after being challenged by the MBE Skyscanner, it shows the potential of governments to influence established hotel distribution practices.

Similarly the impact of the French "Macron Bill", which came into force in August 2015 and outlaws price parity clauses in the contracts between OTAs and hotels is yet to be fully understood. The legislation gives hotels a mandate contract where they will control all pricing and availability for all online reservation platforms and OTAs sales channels (PR Newswire, July 2015). Government intervention may be well intended and aimed at reducing the power of the major OTAs to create a more level playing field for hotels. Again given the current dependency on OTA bookings in hotels, independents in particular, are unlikely to be able to fully exploit any benefits arising out of new legislation for fear of upsetting them. In fact, it is possible that the actions may well further complicate the issue and strengthen the OTAs position.

Current Study Findings

In order to better understand how these changes in distribution are impacting on independent hotels, ten semi-structured interviews were conducted with hotel managers responsible for distribution management from different UK independent hotel companies. The number of hotels in each of companies ranged from between three to twenty-eight.

Nine out of ten respondents stated that the OTA share of the distribution channel mix had increased and in most cases significantly. Six respondents reported they had reduced the number of OTAs that they work with (primarily to Expedia and Priceline) in order to save time and due to non-performance. The actions being taken by hotels to consolidate their OTA partners may inadvertently support the point made in the literature review that the OTA market is becoming a duopoly between Expedia and Priceline.

Many, particularly in London, had also experienced a recent decline in GDS share. Reasons given for the decline in bookings via the GDS included: an increase in room supply in the location which had diluted the share of the corporate market; corporate travellers deciding to book via an OTA and the OTAs themselves actively targeting the corporate traveller for example Expedia through its Egencia programme. One of the respondents rightly pointed out that hotels should probably be asking their corporate customers as to how they would prefer to book, as the decline in GDS distribution channel may well follow that of the traditional leisure travel agent intermediaries.

Only five of the respondents were working with metasearch channels. Of the ones that are using metasearch none had cited having much success in generating significant volumes of direct bookings and had a poor return on investment to date. They did however feel it was important to have a presence on this platform in order to be visible at the early stage of customer search. None of the respondents mentioned working with the so called "gatekeepers" in terms of metasearch however all ten were investing in PPC search advertising primarily with Google.

All respondents had a presence on social media sites such as Facebook and Twitter, however, none saw this as a channel for generating significant volumes of bookings but more as a way to increase brand awareness and customer engagement.

Looking forward all respondents confirmed that their key focus was on increasing bookings through direct channels in particular the Hotel Website. Evidence to date suggests there has been limited success amongst the independent hotel companies reviewed to drive the direct web channel shown by the increase in OTA share in all but one of the cases. Greater success may be achieved through existing channels such as direct telephone bookings as highlighted by one of the respondents. From the interviews it is clear that a significant amount of customers are still calling hotels direct to make a booking.

Focus on this channel may deliver a better return on investment than direct web for independent hotels especially as the rate parity agreements with the OTAs does not apply to telephone bookings.

With seven out of ten respondents reporting increased distribution costs, it is fair to say that distribution costs are an issue for independent hotels. Reasons cited for rising costs were firmly placed on the higher volume of bookings coming via the OTAs. All of the hotel chains reviewed are clearly making efforts to track distribution costs but without a clear and common method of reporting it is difficult to make an assessment as to whether they are calculating the true cost of distribution for each channel.

Having calculated the cost of each distribution channel, a number of the respondents had found that some initiatives used to drive traffic to the hotel's own web channel were actually costing significantly more than the commission paid to OTAs. For example, one of the respondents had experimented with TripConnect a cost per click campaign tool offered by TripAdvisor. In one particular month, the actual cost of the bookings received via this channel came in at an equivalent commission of 40% significantly higher than the average 15-23% paid to the OTAs.

In terms of channel conflict, the hotel distribution managers thought the main causes of conflict between hotels and OTAs were related to:

- Pricing and the constant requirement to offer rate and product parity.
- Bidding on the hotel brand name.
- Constant demands of the OTAs for hotels to offer discounted rates.
- OTAs discounting their commission in order to undercut the hotel.
- Undercutting the hotel in overseas markets.
- Targeting of existing business booked through other channels such as corporate accounts which are primarily received through the GDS.

In terms of strengthening the position of independent hotels when negotiating with their distribution partners, in particular with the OTAs, eight of the hotel distribution partners believed it may be possible to club together to form an alliance. Representation companies such as Leading Hotels of the World and Sabre Synxis could play a part by negotiating with the OTAs on behalf of its partners in a similar fashion to the preferred agreements they have in place with the large booking agents such as American Express or Carlson Wagonlit.

There was certainly mixed feelings amongst the hotel distribution managers when asked about what impact the recent moves by governments to intervene in the OTA/hotel relationship would have on hotel distribution. Three of the respondents actually believed that government intervention to end rate parity agreements would be more advantageous for the

OTAs as it would give them the opportunity to cut their commission rates. System technology in terms of their ability to manipulate rates across different platforms and the size of their customer database was mentioned as the two key reasons that would enable the OTAs to take advantage, if rate parity agreements were scrapped completely.

Overall, the phenomenal growth of the OTAs certainly poses some significant challenges for independent hotel chains due to the rising costs of distribution and channel conflict. The various methods employed to calculate the costs of distribution make it difficult for hotel distribution managers to understand the true cost of each distribution channel which may be resulting in inaccurate decision making. Channel conflict with the OTAs exists and is likely to continue as hotels seem unaware that their actions are the main cause of the conflict. Government attempts to intervene in the contractual relationships between hotels and the OTAs has not been viewed as a positive step by all independent hotel chains with some fearing the abolition of rate parity agreements may actually play further into the hands of the OTAs.

The Impact of UGC on Restaurant Success

By Edward Harvey

Director, Food & Beverage Strategy & Concept Development, Tricon

After 25 years of international food & beverage hospitality experience, **Edward** has managed and developed some of the most successful F&B concepts.

He started his career in 1989 at The Savoy working his way from trainee to deputy banqueting manager. After six years he joined distinguished Swiss chef Anton Mosimann and was responsible for outside high-end events and gained a Royal Warrant.

In 1996 Edward joined Hyatt Carlton Tower, Knightsbridge as Banqueting Manager and was subsequently promoted to Director of Food & Beverage. He gained his first international experience at Grand Hyatt Hong Kong, Park Hyatt Tokyo and Hyatt Regency Macua. When he returned he opened Grissini-London with interior designer David Collins, opened Jamie Oliver's first restaurant and refurbished the famous Rib Room & Oyster Bar.

In 2003 Edward took on a new challenge and opened JW Grosvenor House as Hotel Manager. He established a two Michelin star restaurant with Richard Corrigan and after leading F&B concept development in the Middle East, UK & Ireland, became Corporate Director, Europe - Food & Beverage.

This chapter aims to understand the impact of UGC on restaurant success. The scale and wide-ranging impact of online word of mouth has increased the need for operations to understand and harness customer opinion. This is particularly significant given that research shows consumers perceive peer reviews as one of the most important sources of information during the decision-making process. Restaurateurs need to understand the challenge to manage and anticipate the impact of these re-views given the complexity of creating a restaurant experience. Together with the consumers' perceptions and expectations, they make it difficult to predict how customers will react to a particular dining experience. Many consumers' now consult not only friends and relatives, but also online guides and social media sites. Thus, favourable word of mouth has been for many years a strong means of promotion to the small and medium-size restaurant. However, to date there has been very little research on the potential relationship and impact between user generated content and restaurant success.

Past Research

To understand the impact of UGC on restaurant success it is necessary to understand how consumers choose and evaluate goods and services in the broader sense. Although service marketers are interested in influencing customer choice at the provider level, the decision to patronise a restaurant seldom occurs until after the consumer decides to use the service in the first place (Dorsch et al., 2000). As service providers, the market spends little time considering what motivates the customer's choices. This is meant in the context of the market and not an individual. Restaurants rightly focus on the quality of the service and underline the importance of customer care, but operators seldom think seriously about how consumers make service purchases (Kennedy & Fetter 1999).

Today, during the consumer decision-making process, potential customers can access vast pools of data to help evaluate alternatives. Visitors no longer necessarily enter through the home page of a website and browse as they would a brochure (Schipul, 2006). Increased quantities of information can be both a blessing and a curse. Often the sheer quantity of information available can complicate the decision-making process. Consumers do not have the time or ability to examine all data or compare all options (Bellman 2006). The abundance of alternatives can be over-whelming, leading to confusion, unwise decisions or dissatisfaction with choices made (Smith, Menon & Sivakumar, 2007).

In the off-line world, word-of-mouth recommendations from friends and colleagues play a pivotal role in overcoming the challenges of the web. It helps consumers to know what to believe (Looker, Rockland & Taylor-Ketchum, 2007). As Smith, Menon and Sivakumar (2007) point out, in an information intensive situation, consumers actively seek the opinions of others as a means of managing perceived risks. And while in the past, word-of-mouth implied people talking individually or in small groups by the water cooler, the internet has transformed world-of-mouth into a mass communications media, be it with a predefined group of friends or with thousands of online but connected strangers in an online community (ComScore, 2007). Thus while a dissatisfied customer used to tell ten people of their experience, now thanks to web-based consumer opinion platforms, they can potentially influence thousands of their peers (Hennig-Thurau et al., 2004). By making it easier for consumers to disseminate their point of view and by facilitating access to such opinions, the internet is having a profound effect on how consumers shop (O'Connor, 2008).

Dellarocas (2003) points to anecdotal evidence that consumers are increasingly relying on online peer opinions as inputs in a wide range of decisions as to which products to buy.

Smith, Menon and Sivakumar (2007) claim that consumers prefer such peer recommendations over other forms of input. Because social networks are usually formed between consumers with similar interests and are peer-to-peer, the opinions expressed are perceived to be both relevant and unbiased and are thus more likely to be believed by today's sceptical consumer than advertisements or professional input (Smith, Menon & Sivakumar, 2007). While consumers often turn to such sites to reduce their information overload problem, the proliferation of sites and sheer quantity of user reviews, comments and feedback available may in fact complicate the decision making process (Bellman 2006). In such cases, credibility and trust become even more important and the absence of contextual clues to aid interpretation can be problematic (Dellarocas, 2003). Puri (2007) also highlights the problem of authenticity. Unless appropriate safeguards are in place, participants can post dishonest reviews to enhance their own reputation or tarnish that of their competitors (Dellaro-cas, 2003).

As consumers search online for product information and to evaluate product alternatives, each of these options has the potential to add value for a prospective customer.

Litvin et al., (2008) suggested that tourists' restaurant selections are predominantly influenced by the recommendations of friends or relatives and recommendations of staff at a hotel, with surprisingly few decisions being based on the influence of more formal media such as guide books and advertisements in magazines or newspapers. With the growing popularity of review sites, virtual interactions among online users have become commonplace, which has led some tourism researchers to assert that eWoM plays a vital role in the acquisition and retention of consumers (Litvin et al., 2008; Vermeulen & Seegers, 2009).

The rapid expansion of technological advancements provides an incredible challenge to independent and small and medium-size restaurants. Camilo, Connolly, and Woo (2008, p377) identified the failure to keep up with technological change as a chief reason for the failure of independent restaurants. Certainly it is important to maintain an effective electronic marketing strategy, as highlighted by Kasavana et al., (2010), but the key is to effectively manage the restaurant's online brand.

Current Study Findings

The research involved in depth interviews with 8 restaurant operators responsible for a total of 30 restaurant and two directors of restaurant booking sites. The research had three objectives, these were to understand: (a) what systems and procedures are used to track and monitor user generated content; (b) the impacts of engaging with user generated content and (c) the impact of user generated content on wider organisational strategies. The conclusion of the first research question presented four separate points.

Firstly, all operators monitor UGC at different levels and frequencies. Restaurants linked to hotels benefit from the use of sophisticated e-commerce and social media tools. They also monitor UGC on a daily basis, whereas independent operators approach the monitoring process in a more modest and casual fashion. The viewing is erratic, 'when time allows' and is usually done away from the operation.

Secondly, operators are monitoring a broad range of sources, of which the principal channels are TripAdvisor, Twitter and Facebook. Restaurants linked to hotels view TripAdvisor predominantly although the technology used often provides a UGC aggregator service. Independents tend to source UGC from Twitter and Facebook. The larger operators' decision to focus on TripAdvisor scores, ranking and page position could be due to their predominant customer base being the business and leisure traveller. The monitoring of Twitter and Facebook by the independent operator reflects a market which is mainly locally driven. There are exceptions however where 'big name' 'on-trend' independent restaurants are viewing TripAdvisor because their location is in an area where the client bases are tourist and leisure-driven.

The third point was the importance of processing and using the data. Again, the larger operators and restaurants linked to hotels identified more processes and structure around the review and understanding of UGC. Nevertheless two of the larger independents also used UGC weekly at leadership meetings. All operators conveyed a flow system of information and feed-back from the top down. The comments were all assessed on face value from a standpoint of 'how can we improve?' In the reviewing process, two operators highlighted a system of reward for numbers of reviews, positive comments and names mentioned. To compound this a third operator used a mechanism of reward as an incentive and bribe to improve engagement and scores.

Lastly, responding to UGC was important and needed to be done in a timely manner. Routes for responding differed. Independent operators required the resident manager to respond directly. Larger operators and restaurants linked to hotels responded via a General Manager's personal assistant. A restaurateur from a successful stand-alone restaurant pointed out the dilemma which arose from engaging with Twitter and Facebook. It generated so much communication in return that they could neither cope with nor respond to it all.

The second research question produced two findings. The first found two opposite results from engaging with UGC. The larger operators and restaurants linked to hotels with mechanisms and purpose-built systems engaged and communicated with eWoM in an active fashion. The independents however held back. This being said, two independents with a linked retail operation recognised the use of pictures and Twitter as an important means of engaging with lunch and casual dining customers.

The next point which became clear was that established larger operators were monitoring positions, ranking, scores and customer attitudes but in spite of this were still unsure how to qualify and quantify the impact of UGC. Some offered data as to how numbers had improved but no further evidence emerged to prove the assumptions. The unequivocal response of the independent restaurateurs was 'We can see no noticeable impact.'

The third research question produced two answers as to the impact of UGC on the wider strategies of the organisation. Firstly, the interviewees all understood the importance of managing eWoM and UGC. The larger operators again had in place a strategy linked to goals and objectives in the framework of managing data. Two operators underlined this point by stressing the further financial investment in human capital and e-marketing. On the other hand stand-alone restaurants claimed to understand the importance of UGC yet displayed an alarmingly laid-back attitude to the practice. They talked of giving more attention to engaging and were generally conscious of a need to catch up.

The other theme concerned the operator's plans to use social media and eWoM as a means of communication. All restaurateurs had plans to use social media but in different ways and with different focus. The independent restaurateurs were to be less structured and measured with their plans while the larger operators laid out robust marketing campaigns. The focus was the same for stand-alone restaurateurs whose motivation was to engage and drive local footfall to their establishments. The engagement and communication theme was also underscored by one independent who intended to develop new channels of communication through Pinterest and Instagram, both of which focus on rich picture content in UGC rather than words.

Additional factors which can impact the success of an operation were mentioned by the interviewees. Operators are using UGC in performance reviews. Owners operating at a distance from the restaurant can monitor UGC for trends which affect the business. Rather than employ mystery diners to benchmark standards and performance, UGC is replacing this function.

The study revealed the importance of the use of rich media on websites. Customers searching the web were attracted by photos and videos. It was claimed that Instagram currently has 79 million pictures of food on their site. A difficulty which arises is that the pictures need to be professional in the sense that they are optimised for mobile use. Independent restaurants with limited resources might struggle to achieve this.

Overall, User-Generated Content is recognised by the large chains as certain to play a crucial role in the future and to become more widespread in our day-to-day lives. Once again, the stand-alone restaurant with modest means will struggle to compete in monitoring all of the data and using social media to best effect.

Understanding the Potential of International Sporting Events

•

By Stuart Smith

Brand Home Manager, The Glenmorangie Company
(Previously: Director of Events and Leisure, Gleneagles Hotel)

Stuart has spent over 25 years in the hospitality industry, principally within the luxury hotel sector, both in the UK and Internationally. Stuart began his working life in the hotel industry in Geneva, working as a waiter at the Hotel Des Bergues. He then moved to the Philippines to assist his brother in establishing a bar/restaurant north of Manila.

Returning to the UK he joined the very first Malmaison Hotel based in Leith, Edinburgh before completing a postgraduate MSc in Hospitality Management at Napier University in Edinburgh.

In 1997 he joined the prestigious Gleneagles hotel in Scotland as an Event Co-ordinator and completed his 18 year career there as Director of Events and Leisure. During his tenure at Gleneagles he managed a wide range of events, playing key roles in the delivery of the G8 summit in 2005 and the Ryder Cup in 2014 which saw the world's media descend upon Scotland.

In 2015, Stuart joined Glenmorangie as Brand Home Manager, providing strategic direction and operational management of Glenmorangie House, the company's boutique hotel, and Glenmorangie's Distillery Visitor Centre.

As global communication continues to expand and become faster, constantly breaking down both regional and national barriers, so too does our connection with major sporting events such as the Ryder Cup. No matter where you are in the world, you can be sucked into the sporting cauldron via multiple media channels. Whether you have the good fortune to be present or be watching via whatever device you own, you can see the winning goal being scored, revel in the celebration of a famous victory or hide after an inglorious defeat. With sport, there is an emotional connection – the passion you feel for a team, a player, a country can all come to the fore, teased out by the action and drama played out before you.

These events though have moved on from just being about the pursuit of sporting excellence. Now, they represent business opportunities for a whole spectrum of stakeholders. Governments, through their destination management organisations, realise the value of hosting these events to create awareness and enhance the image of their country. Event suppliers and the tourism trade look for a boost in revenues due to a higher demand for their product. Sponsors look for the association with a great sporting event and the ability to entertain and give their client base an experience they will forever associate with the brand.

The very first golf competition, albeit informal, between Great British and United States professionals was held at Gleneagles in 1921 before the hotel had even opened its doors to guests. 93 years later, the Resort had the opportunity to put both itself and Scotland on the global map by hosting the 40th Ryder Cup between Europe and the USA. Gleneagles, from a sporting and media perspective, was able to dominate the headlines in the latter part of 2014.

Unlike most global sporting events, where the event is hosted at a variety of stadia, often geographically dispersed, the Ryder Cup is played on a single golf course, giving the venue a unique opportunity to promote itself globally. This mass representation within the media gave the resort a huge boost to its awareness but is it feasible to determine how a resort can maximise the benefit that the Ryder Cup will give it? Events such as this have been seen as a strategic opportunity for promotion as well as re-invention, best demonstrated by the 1992 Olympic Games held in Barcelona (Herstein and Berger 2013), when they were able to restyle the image of the city as stylish, trendy and a desirable destination.

The ambition for this chapter is to develop a clear understanding of how to maximise the opportunity presented by hosting a major international sporting event.

Previous Research

Even though over a hundred years old, the idea of a brand being utilised to distinguish the offerings of one company to another has not dramatically altered (Murphy 1998). From a basic perspective, a brand can be seen to be "a name, term, sign, symbol, or design, or a combination of them, intended to identify the goods or services of one seller or group of sellers and to differentiate them from those of competitors." (Kotler 2000). The differentiation between a product and a brand is created by perceived "added values", which play an important part in the purchase decision (Doyle 2002). From a consumer perspective, these added values reduce risk, promote familiarity and create an appeal and attraction. By utilising a brand strategy, companies can gain benefits ranging from creating high levels of consumer loyalty through to higher levels of return compared to competitors (Keller 2002).

The development of the full potential of your brand is based on the relationship that is established with a consumer. In the case of consumer goods, this principally sits with the strength of the product offering. For the services industry, and hotels in particular, it is the service encounter that becomes a critical focal point.

It is much harder for a consumer to feel completely at ease when purchasing a service rather than a product as there is an inherent risk associated with the service not delivering what they would expect. Admittedly, whilst information via multi-media channels is much more prevalent, the view that the brand plays an important role in helping the consumer understand all facets of the service that they may receive, and therefore helps establish a higher level of trust, is significant (Berry 2000). The importance of the employee really does come to the fore, with Punjaisri, Wilson and Evanschitzky (2009) showing that internal branding – the management action of clearly communicating and training their staff to understand and deliver on the ambitions of the business – has a major impact on perceptions of the brand. As Boone (2000) asserts, the employees provide the transformation from brand promise to brand experience for the customer.

However, external influences can and will also have an impact upon the brand image in the mind of the consumer. Typically, these tend to be negative events – financial crashes, terrorism, and natural disasters. However, they can also be positive with mega-events providing one of the best opportunities for an improvement in brand equity. The recent London Olympics are a great example of the belief that mega-events can be the catalyst for change (Swart and Bob 2007). The core ambition of legacy and redevelopment, along with the delivery of a high level sporting event, were key parts of the bid process and post event have created a huge amount of media coverage about whether they have actually been met or not. Whilst the 1995 Rugby World Cup in South Africa was at heart a sporting event, Nelson Mandela used it as an opportunity to show both internal and external parties to South Africa that it was feasible to cut through lifelong held opinions and unite the nation behind a common goal. Similarly the Barcelona Olympics in 1992 used the spotlight as a means of creating a new identity for the city along with an ambitious programme of urban regeneration (Jago et al., 2010). A variety of pressures, such as costs, the variety of stakeholders or even just lack of time combine to ensure that the full potential of these mega events are not always met. Clear and transparent management of these events is therefore critical so that stakeholders do not create any false expectations about what might be delivered through the event. There is a wide variety of the type of impact (Jago et al., 2010) that mega-events can have on a host destination: Economic (foreign exchange earnings, job creation, increased sales for local businesses); Business Leveraging (increased inward investment); Destination branding (setting and changing the image of the host destination); Induced Tourism (increased visitation after the event due to promotion for the event); Legacies (enhanced infrastructure and skill base); and Social (enhanced community spirit and increased sport participation).

Jago et al., (2010) also detail out the potential negative impacts of mega-events. From a hospitality perspective, the two areas of concern would be image, where the brand could possibly be affected due to operational challenges during the event itself (Jago et al., 2003, Coates and Matheson 2009) and security, where the media attention around such an event means it becomes more of a target for terrorism (Nadvi 2008, Donaldson and Ferreira 2007).

From a Gleneagles perspective, the ambition was to ensure that portrayal of the Ryder Cup was utilised to the maximum effect to improve brand perception and awareness (Brown et al., 2004, Chalip et al., 2003) and effectively become a mission in co-branding. Xing and Chalip (2006) showed that this transfer of brand image is feasible and that it works most effectively when there is a link between the nature of the event and the destination.

Although the Ryder Cup has around 200 000 visitors over the course of the tournament, the vast majority will view the event from the comfort of their own living rooms. Mega-events have really come to the fore in terms of TV schedules, really kick-started by the Olympic Games telecast in 1968 (Moreland 2004). These live broadcasts often, along with the sports action, present an opportunity for information about the venue to be distributed around the world. Research by Hede (2005) into the effects of broadcasts on customer perception saw an increase in the favourable perception of Greece further to its hosting of the Olympic Games in 2004. Jago et al., (2010) concludes that in order to achieve maximum potential from the mega-event, focus should be given to "a long term development plan" and "a long term marketing plan" amongst others.

Current Study Findings

Although it has been necessary to look at how the organisation links to the real world and the impact that a major event will have, if we are fully looking to understand the means by which a hotel such as Gleneagles could maximise the opportunity presented by hosting the Ryder Cup, it was important to look too at the strategic management of the organisation.

We now live in a world where change is constant, competition is fierce, technologies advance at dramatic rates and access to knowledge is rapid. How can an organisation face up to all these challenges, particularly organisations that have been established over a number of years and have business models that have offered them success over the years? Is it feasible to create an organisation that allows for strategic resilience – the ability to be able to re-invent yourself at regular intervals in order to avoid stagnation?

Hamel and Valikangas (2003) assert that strategic resilience is not just about allowing a new CEO to enact a turnaround, it is about "having the capacity to change before the case for change becomes desperately obvious." They detail 4 barriers that must be overcome if an organisation is to achieve resilience:

The Cognitive Challenge: This relates to the mind-set of those within the organisation – do they have the ability to avoid denial, be free of hubris and not assume that they or their companies have a given right to the position they currently hold. It is very easy to look at a company that has failed and ask the question "how did they not see that was going to happen" but you only need to look at the Enron Scandal to realise that the ability to ignore the reality of the situation is eminently possible.

The Strategic Challenge: This is the ability to be aware of how your external environment is changing and then having alternative strategies in place to take advantage of these changes.

The Political challenge: this tackles the ability of the organisation to utilise its resources effectively, providing support for new projects whilst also diverting funding from areas that aren't going to succeed.

The Ideological challenge: It is natural that organisations look to put talent and resources into providing the best delivery of their offering to the consumer. However this pursuit of excellence, whilst expected, fails to take on board that this effort becomes wasted if strategic delay is occurring. Essentially, organisations need to develop the ability to be fleet of foot and look to establish an ethos where the ambition is to be able to take advantage of opportunities rather than be forced into renewal through external forces.

From a holistic perspective, the organisation needs to establish what its strategic ambitions are in relation to the major sporting event as this will have an impact on how it looks to present itself to the consumer. The concept of strategic resilience is pertinent here in that it is a means by which established companies can look to change their approach to the market. This change can range from moderate through to radical but no matter the scale of the change, these adjustments should feed into how a brand presents itself. Within this the idea of managing the brand as an asset, leveraging its worth in order to further develop business goals, is core.

A mega-event, such as the Ryder Cup, can act as a catalyst for change. For the organisation, in this case Gleneagles, it presents an opportunity to build on its strategic ambitions, opening up potentially new markets. For the employee, having the opportunity to showcase their skills to a worldwide audience can be exhilarating and for the potential consumer it can create a level of awareness and an initial emotional connection through the concept of co-branding whilst for those already aware of the property, this emotional connection may well be deepened. However, it is worth considering too that there is an inherent risk within the hosting of the Ryder Cup. If, for any reason, there are negatives emerging from the event – weather delays, poor event co-ordination, even a poor performance from either team – there is the possibility that this could have a detrimental impact upon how the consumer will come to reflect upon Gleneagles post Ryder Cup.

The opportunity that the Ryder Cup presented for Gleneagles will ultimately be led by the image perceived by consumers. However, it has to be recognised that Gleneagles only had a certain level of influence over the consumer during the Ryder Cup, when the potential positives and negatives of co-branding with the Ryder Cup emerged.

Disintermediation of Hotel Distribution

By Clinton Campbell

Director of Revenue, Apex Hotels Limited

Clinton Campbell was born and raised in South Africa and attended the International Hotel School, Durban, graduating in 2000 with a diploma cum laude. Clinton relocated to the UK in 2002 and worked in front office operational roles until 2008 when he started his career in revenue management and is currently the Revenue Director at Apex Hotels. In 2015 he completed his Master's Degree at the University of Strathclyde, Glasgow in Hospitality and Tourism Leadership and specialises in the commercial functions of Revenue, Marketing and Sales.

How do hotels, in particular revenue managers, deliver ongoing increases in both profitability and market share in the future? The landscape in which hotels distribute their inventory has changed dramatically over the last decade and technology will play a significant part in delivering continued success. As the use of the internet has grown, customer behaviour has changed and the sale of hotel inventory has shifted from off-line to online. Online Travel Agencies have jumped at the opportunity to sell hotel inventory for hefty commissions which is digging in to hotel profitability.

Customer journeys these days are tracked on more than two dozen websites prior to making a purchase and hotels are desperate that the final purchase is made on their own website. As this offers the best information available about a guest and the cheapest direct transaction cost. The majority of purchases are being made through the OTAs which has been made possible through the hotels engaging with them and providing suitable technology to give them full access to all their inventory. This chapter seeks to determine if hotels are able to disintermediate from certain channels and influence customers to book on their own hotel websites.

Previous Research

It is suggested that economics is the driving force for the changes in distribution (Carroll & Siguaw, 2003). The cost of distributing rooms through Online Travel Agents (OTAs) can range from "10% - 50% of top line revenue" (Green & Lomanno, 2012, p. 17). We also know that engaging with new distribution channels can have a positive impact on the performance of the hotel. Hotels are now being exposed on a number of different platforms of Social Media. Responding to TripAdvisor's comments, posting updates on Facebook and sending pictures via Twitter are not something that hotels are always geared up for.

TripAdvisor has developed in to more than just a social platform and is now one of the larger Meta Booking Engines (MBEs). "Meta-search (and booking) engines search the online travel agency sites, as well as supplier sites, thereby adding an additional level of intermediary function" (Granados, et al., 2008). This could be a good thing for hotels as it gives them a new opportunity to participate in winning guests using pay per click advertising to display the hotel directly.

When hotels first started to use OTAs it was for the purpose of adding incremental revenue for rooms that would have otherwise been unsold. However, the OTAs volume has continued to grow and growth in direct web traffic has been stagnant.

Price can be an influencer in search results and we know that both OTAs and MBEs use a hotel's price to rank a hotel on their websites which will often have a direct impact on the visibility of that hotel and as such "hotels are faced with a trade-off between obtaining a desirable position and paying a high commission fee" (Ling, et al., 2014, p. 243). In 2009 Expedia dropped Choice Hotels' inventories from its websites after a breakdown in negotiations (Lee, et al., 2013). There was blame on both sides of the table, and there was much criticism from some of the hotel owners that they were losing business. One month later Choice Hotels signed a new deal which indicates that the impact was detrimental to their hotels. Had the impact not been bad, Choice Hotels could have remained aggressive and dictated more favourable terms with Expedia. Does this mean that hotels are bound to the OTAs? When speaking to hoteliers today many would argue that they can't walk away from the larger OTAs (Booking.com and Expedia). Some independent hotels have opted to fully embrace the power the OTAs offer and use them fully to distribute their inventory online. They claim to be able to reach customers they would not otherwise have been able to target directly.

Current Study Findings

A total of eight semi-structured interviews with industry experts from independent hotels in London were undertaken to establish the relationship hotels have with their distribution channels and also to see if hotels could disintermediate while maintaining performance.

Most of the respondents indicated that they thought their properties had a very straightforward form of connectivity with their distribution channels. The most common CRS supplier was Sabre with their SynXis platform. When asking about the relationship that each hotel had with their intermediaries, the results differ by specific channel. The feeling was that GDS was a relatively easy channel to manage as there was not much involvement from the revenue managers themselves. The OTAs commanded the majority of their time and also appeared to give them frustrations about having to check if they were in fact offering parity on the rates. FIT only required contracting once a year but had to be manually entered in to the PMS (Property Management System). None of the revenue managers themselves did this task. When asked about how some of these challenges were different to a few years ago there was consensus that previously the OTA channel was used to sell last-minute, or unsold distressed inventory and the terms were generally dictated to them by the hotels. The opposite is now the case.

Most respondents indicated that they wanted to share their distribution across the channels while maintaining a reasonable commission level. Ultimately they would prefer a lower commission rate but accepted that that won't necessarily happen. Responses were also aligned in that they didn't want the intermediaries to target their direct and corporate customers. Intermediaries are currently bidding on the individual hotels' key words on search engines like Google and Bing. This forces the hotels to increase their bidding prices to compete, to ensure that some customers are able to book directly at the hotel where very little cost is incurred.

Channel dilution was expressed as a main concern by some of the respondents. They felt that the OTAs had now saturated the leisure market and were now actively targeting the corporate market. There was concern as this is predominantly a GDS source of business which has a lower cost than the OTAs. When questioned about the impact on the guest, there was acknowledgement that booking through and managing stays on OTA platforms could be easier for the guests.

There was agreement that the growth and change in hotel distribution has been good for customers. The platforms that the public can use are easy to navigate. The respondents did acknowledge that they would now be willing to support the customers more if they did book direct on the website or on the telephone. When questioned as to why this was not done before, the general response was that they didn't think they had a need to do anything differently and struggled with the correct resource of time and money to implement similar practices to the OTAs.

Among the respondents, there was a general lack of knowledge or understanding around the actual cost of a booking through each channel. Likewise, there was limited useful information that they could provide about the revenue associated with each channel in the primary and ancillary revenue streams. One respondent mentioned that their approach to measuring was of top level costs and highlighted that there may be flaws when looking purely at the profit and loss accounts - "The P&L only has one line for commission, so the rest of the distribution costs are scattered across about four other lines under different areas of sales and marketing." There was consensus that the direct website channel was the cheapest but this sometimes didn't take account of the costs associated with driving traffic to the website. To simply measure the individual transaction cost on the hotel's website is not comparable to that of a complete intermediary commission. There was better analysis done at that time looking at the fees and commission when deciding if a new channel or partner should be introduced. They wouldn't continue to pay a higher commission rate if the channel wasn't able to produce the required amount of business in the right seasons and not all in the high season.

Generally there was acceptance that various channels had their own unique selling points as summarised in the following:

Direct Hotel Website
- Cheapest channel that the hotel could control and make changes to very rapidly.
- This channel produced business across all days of the week with a decent length of stay.
- There was little knowledge in terms of costs associated with indirect costs of driving volume to this channel.
- Some hotels used Metasearch to support volume through to the hotels' websites.

GDS
- Generally the cost on this channel was not perceived to be an issue for the hotels. Most hotels paid a single transaction fee followed, on occasion, by commission on non-contracted rates.
- As this was a corporate market it produced mainly midweek.
- This channel was more complex to manage as updates had to be submitted to a third party to implement.
- Lead time here was from 6 weeks prior to arrival.

OTAs
- While the actual percentage mix varied in all hotels, there was agreement that the growth in this channel was the highest.
- Good channel for driving a lot of volume where needed, but most expensive channel in terms of direct commission.
- OTA extranets are flexible to support hotels for specific sales, but the content is managed by the OTA account managers.
- Lead time by specific OTAs varies. Expedia in particular with their package holidays has a longer lead in of about 60 days. Booking.com lead times were shorter. Booking.com had also launched, via their mobile app, a platform for guests to make discounted same day reservations without a credit card.

While conducting this research it was very clear that distribution was a topic that all hotels were trying to understand and control fully. The industry does not support any benchmarking data at channel cost level and the reason is considered to be because of the lack of an agreed configuration of data recording at property level.

In terms of overall impact on performance in the hotels, none of the respondents said they weren't happy with the overall performance of their channel mix. There was agreement that hotels seemed to spend significantly more time working on distribution trying to control it which is very different from about five years ago when each channel was left to simply produce what it could – and hotels generally needed the most channels they could find.

There was agreement that hotels had increased resource in online channels once the realisation that the traditional FIT models were decreasing. One respondent confirmed that they employed a sales manager specifically to drive that traffic. Technology in hotels supported this new drive and systems that could offer the best two way integration between the OTA and hotel were generally installed giving OTAs full availability to hotel inventory. More recently, two respondents admitted that they had begun to reduce the number of OTAs they work with leaving only Booking.com and Expedia. While this may reduce the number of accounts to manage, particularly culling those that produce very little revenue, it strengthened the power of the two largest OTAs by eliminating their competitors for them. Low cost channels like direct websites were identified as being underutilised. Hotels admitted that there was an opportunity to make more use of this channel, but they did not have confidence that a sufficient volume of business would be generated.

To conclude, looking at the ability of hotels to disintermediate and maintain performance, the interviews supported this as an option. However, there are caveats attached that hotels will have to adhere to in order to maintain overall performance. If hotels want to dramatically change their mix then the appropriate amount of time should be allowed to manage this. Additionally, hotels need to review and analyse new channels individually looking at what they can deliver and examining whether they overlap in strategy with any other channels. Technology will play a large part in controlling distribution in the future as the trend to move all purchasing to online channels will continue. Improving internal understanding and knowledge around digital e-commerce will be vital if true comparisons are to be made between a hotel's website and the OTAs. The intermediaries are constantly improving their booking platforms to engage with guests and increase conversion, which leads to hotels coming under pressure to do likewise. While many hotels would like to reduce their use of OTAs, many simply cannot at this time without negatively impacting their overall financial performance.

Drowning in the Red Ocean: Hotels, Technology and the Customer

By Peter Stack

Head of Asset Management, Amaris Hospitality

Peter Stack is currently the Head of Asset Management for Amaris Hospitality. Previously, as Regional Operations Manager for Jurys Inn, Peter succeeded in various roles including UK North where he was responsible for 15 hotels and more recently London, with responsibilities extending to include the re-branding of Jurys Chelsea and Jurys Islington hotels to Hilton DoubleTree, and for Jurys Heathrow to Hilton Garden Inn. Peter is a graduate from the Shannon Collage of Hotel Management where he completed his studies in 1995. In 2014 Peter completed an Executive Masters in Hospitality and Tourism Leadership, led by Strathclyde Business School and more recently completed the Hotel Real Estate Investments and Asset Management program with Cornell University.

A red ocean strategy focuses on gaining a greater share of existing demand. As the market space gets crowded, prospects for profits and growth reduce. Products become commodities and cut throat competition turns the ocean bloody red. A blue ocean strategy, in contrast, focuses on accessing untapped market space and creating demand. Those adopting a blue ocean strategy do not use the competition as their benchmark, but innovate through creating added value for the customer.

This chapter sets out to determine if technology and co-production techniques are significantly influencing the hospitality industry and if the industry is utilising self-service technology to improve the service experience. The UK mid-market hotel sector is becoming increasingly crowded and as a result it is vital for hotel brands to create points of differentiation. With the growing strength of OTAs and increasing consumer acquisition costs along with the emergence of new brands, hotels are becoming increasingly commoditised and carving out a clear identity is vital to gain increased loyalty and brand awareness. To combat this, hotels are using technology to differentiate their hotel brand from competitors. A number of new technology focused hotel brands have recently emerged like Citizen M, W Hotel and Marriott's new venture with IKEA, Moxy Hotels. Wider than this, a number of hotel brands are increasingly introducing customer facing technology to create a competitive advantage. Hotel brands like Novotel, Premier Inn and Travel Lodge are moving away from the traditional service experience one would usually expect from a hotel by introducing self-service technologies (SSTs) like self-check-in. While SSTs are not new to many industries like banks, supermarkets, airlines and so on, this is a very recent change to the hospitality industry and as a result raises a number of strategic questions.

Previous Research

There is a lot of literature claiming that co-production techniques are the next real competitive advantage for organisations (Peters et al., 2012, Auh et al., 2007, Bendapudi et al., 2003). Ramirez (1999) and Bendapudi et al., (2003) propose that businesses today are increasingly acting as facilitators which allow consumers to create their own product or service experience. This is in contrast to firms creating a service which consumers purchase. There are a number of reasons proposed as to why customers co-produce. Bendapudi et al., (2003) state it reduces labour costs and as a result reduces pricing for customers. Hsieh et al., (2004) supports this logic but add that it also improves service performance. Auh et al., (2007) lists a number of benefits customers can gain by co-producing including choice, lower prices, greater discretion, more opportunity, shorter waiting times and the ability to customise. Peters et al., (2012) looks at it differently and proposes customers engage in co-production for fun, the opportunity to create an experience or for the sense of accomplishment.

Benapudi et al., (2003) work demonstrates that the benefits of co-production techniques has evolved from more than the widely accepted economic benefits like improved productivity and efficiency which typically lower prices for the co-producer. His research shows that co-production techniques have the ability to increase competitive advantage by improving customer satisfaction. This view is supported by Hsieh et al., (2004) who when defining the importance of customer participation includes that it has the ability to have a number of positive impacts for an organisation such as improved service performance, service quality perception and likelihood to re-purchase.

Self Service Technology (SST) is defined as "where customers deliver service themselves using some form of a technological interface" (Beatson 2006, p853) a definition supported by (Robertson et al, 2011). The introduction of SST is changing the customer business relationship as customers use SST to deliver service for themselves replacing the personal service interaction (Meuter et al., 2000; Beatson et al., 2006; Lema, 2009). The benefits for customers who participate in generating their own service through SSTs are well documented including privacy, convenience, speed, sense of control and the ability to customise (Beatson et al.,2006; Brown et al., 2011).

Brown et al., (2011, p26) states one of the driving forces behind this change is the internet which is changing consumers behaviour as they become "more accustomed to a variety of choices, mass customisation and immediate service".

Organisations experience a number of challenges when implementing SST which for the purpose of this dissertation are categorised into two categories: challenges created by the removal of service personnel from the process and challenges created directly by SST implementation. Some of the challenges created by the removal of service personnel include technology's ability to resolve problems, customisation which can be better anticipated by service personnel and technology's lack of ability to exceed customer expectations by delighting the customer (Meuter et al., 2000; Brown et al., 2011). Some of the challenges presented by SST implementation as already highlighted may mean "service recovery is not yet achievable with SSTs" (Meuter et al., 2000, page 60) an issue which becomes a greater challenge when Robertson et al (2012) proposes customers are less likely to self-blame when issues occur while utilising SST. Robertson et al., (2012) proposes a solution for these issues when suggesting service guarantees should be offered as a way to overcome these challenges while other research suggest a mixed approach solution to SST implementation by retaining elements of personal service (Beatson et al., 2006; Reinders et al., 2008). Meuter et al., (2000, p60) suggests another challenge when highlighting that users are becoming more sophisticated and as a result "SST satisfaction is likely to be fleeting". This implies that SST needs to be more robust than simply installing a convenient machine and needs to create real value for the customer. This challenge is supported by Brown et al., (2011) who highlights that organisations are struggling to incorporate technology into corporate strategy and are struggling to create value from implementing SST.

According to Beatson et al., (2006, p854) "Hotels are traditionally high service areas" and "customer satisfaction is linked to overall performance" (p856). However there are many views that customer service delivery is changing (Lema, 2009; Kim et al., 2011) and claims that SST is changing service delivery by replacing the personal interaction. Some of the service issues SST may resolve are summarised by Meuter (2000, p51) including "Employee response to service delivery failure, employee response to customer needs and requests and unprompted and unsolicited actions by the employee".

Meuter et al., (2000) identifies that enjoyment and control are the two most influencing factors for customers when engaging with SST but factors which achieve the highest levels of satisfaction for customers using SSTs are time saving and the fact that it did its job. These satisfaction factors according to Meuter et al., (2000) and Kim et al., (2011) are basic and may only achieve customer satisfaction for a short period of time. Given the importance of customer satisfaction in the hospitality industry, will SST be a suitable substitution for personal service or will it evolve more like Beatson's (2006) claim that "in a hotel context personal service still remains very important for assessments of satisfaction" (p 853).

It is evident from the literature reviewed that not all customers will engage with SSTs to the same level as highlighted by Beatson et al., (2006) who advises hotels should be taking into consideration how consumer requirements and expectations may differ. As a result this chapter aims to build on current literature to understand hotel customers' different expectations of a hotel experience and if the hotel industry is in a position to fully embrace SST.

Current Study Findings

In total four CEO interviews, three staff focus groups and two customer focus groups were conducted. A total of 18 hotel staff and 8 hotel guests attended the focus group interviews. Employees were selected based on their industry experience and only regular hotel customers were selected so their hotel experience would add value to the data.

At the beginning of each interview participants were asked to rank in order of importance their top ten features when selecting a hotel from a list of 20 items. The following 6 items received the most points from the focus groups:

(1) value for money (2) staff friendliness (3) comfortable bed (4) free high quality Wi-Fi (5) good breakfast (6) fast and friendly check-in.

These features are the hygiene factors when selecting a hotel and will have a direct impact on satisfaction.

Features which received the lowest points included the smart bedroom concept, smart TVs and self-service check-in.

When co-production or SST techniques were discussed, participants felt these would be appropriate or acceptable for budget hotels and not for full service hotels. The main reason for this is that when customers are paying a certain level there is a service expectation. When discussing the check-in experience, interviewees did not associate co-production's ability to remove repetitive procedural tasks with freeing up an employee's time to focus on customer engagement. Utilising technology to make the customer a partial employee was viewed by the hotels interviewed as negatively impacting service levels as opposed to removing basic tasks and allowing employees the time to improve the customer experience.

Other views were that organisations would use technology to reduce staffing levels and in turn payroll costs. As a result, the view was that it would result in a reduced customer service experience. All hotel Executives agreed that technology replacing employees was not a realistic option in a hotel environment; however, Citizen M confirmed it had reduced the number of front line staff but in doing so had changed the employee role and improved customer satisfaction.

When discussing how technology is changing the customer service experience, Executives discussed the importance of a good customer database. By this they were referring to recording repeat customer preferences so it could be used to enhance a customer's future stay. According to Executives utilising this information to achieve customer loyalty, it is now an industry priority due to the rise in OTAs and associated commission costs. However the majority of interviewees stated that the customer information quality is still generally poor and as a result cannot be used consistently to improve customer service. Some of the reasons for this included too much manual intervention, poor compatibility with external systems, poor staff knowledge and ability. In particular the customers interviewed expressed frustration around lack of recognition, poor service consistency and poorly managed loyalty programs.

Also in terms of customer service experience, hotel customers were extremely frustrated with the fact Wi-Fi was not free. This view was echoed by hotel employees who stated it was a source of a significant number of complaints received. The industries failure to react to and meet customers' Wi-Fi expectations is an example of the industry's technology response-lag.

The majority of current technology investments mentioned by Executives during the interviews were non-customer facing. Instead Executives appear to be focusing on improving current IT systems to overcome current industry challenges. This research highlights that the majority of Hotel Executives either do not view customer facing technology as having the ability to create a competitive advantage or that it is not an industry priority due to current priorities to survive. There is also a view that customer facing technology may not create value but instead commoditise the hotel product resulting in the devaluing of the product as customers become more price focused. Participants claimed the industry is not a technology leader and as a result needs to invest more in people development. A lack of knowledge is suggested as a reason for this view however, another explanation is that the industry has a more short term and tactical approach due to owner and operator structures. The industry is investing technology capital into areas including property management systems to improve quality databases, and revenue management systems to combat competition and optimise revenue. The strategy is not investing in new technology to achieve competitive advantage, but into current systems to combat competition and industry challenges. However this strategy appears to be struggling to achieve this consistently due to poor technology. Hotels are unable to utilise customer databases effectively due to data quality and as a result regular hotel customers interviewed demonstrated frustration with the lack of recognition. In addition, hotel employees stated they couldn't guarantee to meet customers' requests for upgrades etc. as the systems couldn't guarantee it.

This technology-lag also appeared evident in the industry's ability to achieve mass customisation. The current focus remains on a traditional way to customise a repeat customer's stay by employees gathering hotel customer preferences. This method is a labour intensive reactive way to customise and the results from the customer focus groups show it is failing to achieve consistency and meet their needs. This view of customers wanting everything done for them is challenged by Citizen M's view that customers want to customise themselves so they can personalise their own hotel stay. Similar to the Wi-Fi issue hotels are facing today, customer customisation expectations could be changing and as a result, the industry's failure to meet these expectations could result in a similar level of future complaints.

Overall, this study suggests that the traditional role of the employee needs to change from a procedural focus to an experience focus. To achieve this, the industry needs to proactively and strategically engage with customer facing technology. Technology is a part of everyday life, customers are accustomed to technology and as a result may be increasingly likely to engage with SST. All participants agreed that the requirements of Generation Y would be different as they are more technology aware and as a result are more likely to engage with SST. The majority of participants acknowledge that the industry is currently not preparing for this future market and as a result may struggle to meet Generation Y's expectations.

Service Recovery in the Hotel Industry

By Jonathan Walker

Managing Director, No.15 Great Pulteney

Jonathan studied Hotel Management for four years and spent the early part of his career in Edinburgh at the Caledonian and Balmoral Hotels. He then moved to Marriott as Hotel Operations Manager and later to IHG where he spent 14 years working in many key roles.

During his tenure at IHG he opened two hotels in Birmingham and London and managed large hotels at Heathrow and in central London. Later Jonathan moved to work as Area Director, and then to Operations Support Director for UK and Europe.

Jonathan then moved to Operations Director at The Hotel Collection and then established his own Hotel Management Consultancy. For the last year he has fulfilled a career ambition of investing in a private hotel and is now Managing Director of No.15 Great Pulteney in Bath, a stunning boutique hotel that opened in December 2016.

Jonathan is an Acorn Award Winner and whilst at IHG received a Catey, Hotel of the Year award, General Manager of the year and a number of corporate awards.

The hospitality industry, unlike manufacturing, relies heavily on service quality. For this reason, it will indefinitely be at risk of service failure, resulting predominantly from human error. Service recovery however, offers a rare opportunity for hoteliers to deliver a unique selling point and differentiation. This is increasingly important since the rise of social and business media, which has provided a platform for guests to exchange views on service performance with immediate effect. Websites such as 'TripAdvisor' (founded in 2000) have positioned the power of knowledge with the consumer, who has an increasingly sophisticated, well-informed outlook on the industry. Social media has the potential to determine the success or failure of company processes, including service recovery, at an unprecedented rate. The threat of new entrants to the hotel market, such as 'Airbnb', also heightens the competitive pressures.

The purpose of this chapter is twofold. Primarily the research aims to identify best practice for service recovery within the hotel industry, contrasting this against the context of current practice. However, a vital element of identifying best practice will be the exploration of employee empowerment; it's potential to improve customer perceptions of the recovery process, and the challenges preventing successful implementation of this leadership approach.

Previous Research

For customers, a service failure is an occurrence where part of the process affecting the experience is broken, bringing about negative emotions Palmer et al., (2000). Service recovery is the process and activity, which a company engages into, in order to handle the complaint.

The success of recovery from the customer's viewpoint is how they evaluate the 'justice or fairness of the recovery efforts and the compensation' Siu et al., (2013).

When service fails and there is perceived inequality, this can have a financial impact on the organisation's bottom line (Carson et al., 1998). Besides the financial implications, there are alternative reasons why effective service recovery is important. As Hart et al., (2000, p149) realise "the battle for market share is won, not by analysing demographic trends, rating points and other global measures, but rather by pleasing customers".

Social media has also heightened the importance of service recovery since poor service is immediately broadcast via online platforms such as twitter and trip advisor. Whilst there is conjecture around the credibility of social media and its impact on hotel bookings and revenues, there is acceptance that user-generated content has become an important point of reference. Importantly, dissatisfied customers typically complain to 9-10 other people about service imperfections, while satisfied customers typically express contentment to only 4-5 others (Brown & Reingen, 1987).

The Service Recovery Paradox (SRP) is defined as where a consumer's post-failure level of satisfaction exceeds that of their satisfaction, had the failure not occurred (McCollough and Bharadwaj, 1992). Krishna et al., (2014) promotes SRP as a phenomena, and believes the theory is proven when "recoveries can build more loyalty than in no failure conditions". He suggests there are two critical factors impacting the degree of SRP: the magnitude of service failure and the degree of consumer generosity. Generosity is linked to: tolerance, an understanding nature and empathy. It could be argued that, since those working in the service industry cannot control how generous their customers are, they must instead consider the one variable which they can control – service failure magnitude. In other words, SRP can be an effective outcome, but only if efforts are taken to minimize the service failure first. This argument is linked to the concept of trust. If customers trust that efforts were made to minimize the failure in the first place, and the failure is also confronted by excellent service recovery, SRP is likely to occur. Krishna et al., (2014) state that, "it is a well-known fact that service recovery has a great impact on trust". However, alternative literature exists to challenge SRP (McCollough et al., 2000, Chihyung, Ki-Joon, and Shankin, 2006). These academics highlight how the positive impact of SRP diminishes after more than one failure, and how SRP is extremely difficult to achieve where loss impacts a person emotionally in comparison to simply being a loss of time, money or physical attributes. Although, it would be dangerous to wholeheartedly advocate support either for or against SRP, the implementation of a procedural approach to service recovery is suggested as a positive consideration for businesses. It is particularly advocated when the failure is not severe, where there is no prior failure and when the consumer perceives that the failure is genuine Magnini et al., (2007).

Traditional service recovery techniques were built upon the aforementioned definition of service recovery as a systematic planned process (Zemke and Bell, 1990), thus focusing on the tangible recovery efforts performed by the supplier, as opposed to the interaction between the supplier and the customer. Examples are discounts, refunds, replacements, free gifts and apologies (Hoffman and Kelley 2000; Tax et al., 998). However, modern day hospitality organisations are required to be increasingly flexible in their approach to service recovery. As Hart et al., (2000, p150) note, 'unlike manufacturers that can adjust the inputs and machinery until products are uniformly perfect, service companies cannot escape variation'. Hence, the 'take it or leave it' compensation approach may not be suited to future customer needs. In light of this social shift, it appears reasonable that employees may require to be empowered in order to bestow fiscal and informational resources required to tend to consumer needs (Spreitzer. 1996).

In its most basic definition, empowerment is understood to be the granting of power and decision making authority. Empowering employees moves decision-making authority down the hierarchy and grants employees the ability to make decisions. According to Lovelock and Wirtz (2010), "employee empowerment is one of the most effective tools to satisfy and service customers". Kim et al., (2004) confirm that empowerment allows employees to have more flexibility and responsibility with respect to various customers' needs. Empowered employees are able to resolve customer problems more rapidly by creating solutions themselves.

A reputation for customer service extends beyond current customers and starts to create new customers as word spreads about the company's quick responsive actions.

However, there are difficulties in training an employee to accept empowerment and responsibility. As Hart et al., (2000) state, empowerment requires decision making and rule-breaking – exactly what employees have been conditioned against. Moreover there could be a reluctance to transfer responsibility if 'middle –level managers' read it as an erosion of their own authority and worth.

For empowered employees, the company's whole culture surrounding the team and business needs to encompass empowerment. To develop an individual or team in service recovery empowerment is restrictive and somewhat impossible if, in other parts of the business, there is still a culture of rigorous control. This is an all or nothing approach.

Current Study Findings

The current study involved the undertaking of a survey of customers alongside a programme of qualitative research with hotel employees and general managers. The main sources of dissatisfaction with the service recovery efforts of hotels were the speed of response and the use of rigid policies and procedures when addressing complaints. However, a contradictory argument also arose. Some interviewees suggested that the approach to handling service issues lacked consistency, even within the same hotel brand, and that this was also central to their dissatisfaction. There is therefore a paradox between empowerment and personal service recovery, and a consistent but fair approach. However, there was general consensus that positive experiences resulted from employees who appeared knowledgeable and apologetic, and who reacted speedily and with empathy.

From a consumer's perspective, speed of resolution did appear to be the most important factor. Where resolving the complaint resulted in a time delay, caused by incompetence, and being passed from one employee to another, as a result of weak empowerment, there was dissatisfaction. It is also the case that solving the complaint quickly, and keeping it 'in house', prevents the complaint from escalating within the social media arena. Moreover, quick responses have financial benefits.

In terms of communication, it can be broken down into three key elements: communication to the customer during the service recovery situation, post-customer communication, and internal communication to record and track complaints. However, the best communication is where no communication is required in the first instance. In other words, where the service provider pre-empts the customer's specific requirements and recognises the need for the recovery to take place. Premier Inn's 'sleep guarantee' was identified by all stakeholders as being best practice within the industry. The assurance of a good night's sleep together with a money back guarantee is seen a bold customer service promise.

General Managers referred to empathy as being critical, positioning the term as seeing service issues "through the customer's eyes". In order to be empathetic, general managers positioned employee confidence as "vital" to achieving effective service recovery results. It all comes back to employee confidence in dealing with difficult situations and being able to make smart decisions. This is achieved through the correct corporate culture, trust from management and training.

Among respondents, where training existed, sessions focused on identifying signs of customers who had complaints by watching for specific body language and signs. It also focused on the importance of listening, capturing relevant notes, showing empathy, and speed and communication. However, the training in service recovery is inconsistent across hotels. The attitude of corporate hotels appears correct since they have strong training programmes. However these are not aimed at educating new recruits and from the research it showed that where companies did deliver service recovery training, there was little attempt to review success or revisit at a later date. Corporate hoteliers more commonly trained around defined guidelines and processes, however there were generally very few written processes or models linked to a service recovery approach. In privately owned hotels, the emphasis is on employing strong front of house staff that can make decisions and act speedily supported by the personal involvement of the general manager and owner.

Results revealed varied attitudes to employee empowerment as a strategy to improve service recovery. Of the 35 customers questioned, 21 were passed to more than one employee. These results clearly highlight an area for improvement. Many general managers and employees discussed the ceiling of empowerment and some even quoted figures, for example £100, at which empowerment stops and the employee must consult somebody more senior. As speed of resolution is critical, employee empowerment is seen as being essential for successful service recovery. Empowered employees can resolve the issues promptly giving confidence to the customer. Good empowerment can lead to highly motivated and committed employees and can lead to being an employer of choice. This approach undoubtedly takes organizational commitment from senior management, much time, and often-cultural change. It is not a strategy, which can be switched on and off.

Empowerment must also be considered from an employee's point of view. In theory, it seems like a great strategy, however many employees feel more comfortable with having parameters on compensation, and guidelines for their responses. Sometimes employees are the impediment to allowing empowerment to benefit service recovery. However, it was often cited that management fear was the reason the company didn't benefit from empowerment. Managers reported of how they feared that empowerment would result in high costs since employees "throw money at problems". High labour turnover was another common reason given for why empowerment was difficult to obtain. Furthermore, keeping employee empowerment alive through coaching was an obstacle due to the necessary time commitment.

Historically, service recovery has always formed part of hotel processes. However, the approach to service recovery must change with new generations of customers. Where the hotelier may have, in the past, treated customers with the contempt of 'Basil Fawlty', in today's connected society this would result in a public relations disaster. Modern hoteliers realise the importance of effective service recovery, and its impact on perceptions of overall service quality. Their own positive experiences with companies such as 'The John Lewis Partnership', 'Naked Wines' and 'Amazon', and their negative experiences, notably from UK Utility providers, have enabled reflection and consideration of best practice within their own businesses.

This research has illustrated how, within a hyper-competitive environment, effective service recovery provides scope for hotels and brands to distinguish themselves and establish a sustained competitive advantage. Core to the successes of any business is consistency, and hence companies must deliver a structured approach, which will embed great service recovery into company culture. This is likely to involve clear messaging, communication and relevant training. Ideally this structured approach would introduce the concept of great service recovery to employees early in their career, and develop this throughout the employee life cycle.

There is also a role for empowerment. However in practice, effective empowerment still requires some specific guidelines for employees to work within. Whilst this may not meet the idealism of pure empowerment, it is a necessary compromise to deliver optimum success. Some customers also felt that where employees balanced empowerment with some sense of boundaries, a fairer result was given.

Owners and management must consider how their opinion of front-line employees impacts service recovery prospects. Without trust, empowerment is impossible; and as has been stated above, without empowerment, at least to some degree, great service recovery is not likely.

Hotel Loyalty and Generation Y

By Simon Davis

Area General Manager, Apex Hotels Ltd

Simon Davis commenced his career in Zimbabwe completing his initial industry training at the Meikles Hotel in Harare and the Victoria Falls Hotel, both members of the Leading Hotels of the World consortium. He graduated with a Diploma in Hotel Management and moved to the UK in 2002 working in a number of operational roles until 2007 when he was appointed his first General Manager position with Arora Hotels.

Joining Apex Hotels in 2011 he has held General Management positions in London before recently taking up the role of Regional Director for the Scottish Central Belt. In 2014 he completed his MSc (Distinction) in Hospitality and Tourism Leadership at the University of Strathclyde in Glasgow.

Generation Y is quickly emerging to become the largest consumer group in the world. To ensure continued growth in market share, hotel companies are exploring how they can attract this generational cohort. Taking into consideration the plethora of hotel and destination choice that is available to this tech-savvy cohort, it is of interest to examine Generation Y's loyalty to hotel brands and how this may influence change in the hospitality industry over the years ahead.

Previous Research

Bush, et al., (2004), characterize the Generation Y cohort as a market segment that possibly creates the biggest challenge, describing them as defiant to conventional marketing campaigns and hard to attract and keep as loyal customers. Data reported by Greenburg (2011), reflected only 3% of the Generation Y as loyal to a particular brand. Sebor (2006) and Wood (2004), argue that this generational cohort are notoriously disloyal to brands and are difficult to secure repeat purchasing transactions from, in contrast to generation X consumers that are very committed and loyal to brands (Richie,1995). A recent hospitality study by Bridge. Over (2014), found that 70% of millennial consumers are less brand loyal than previous generations, with the number rising to 81%, when considering hotel brands. Furthermore when ranking the selection criteria by importance, Generation Y rated a loyalty program as the least important metric this generational cohort consider when making a hotel brand purchasing decision.

Generation Y cohort contain a distinctive outlook towards brands, which is unique to their predecessors. Markow (2005), articulates how Gen Y consumers are exceedingly concerned as to how others perceive them, due to the social grouping and community formation in which they have grown up. Noble, et al., (2009) state that they are attracted to purchase products, which project a representation that mirrors a likeness to themselves. In this consumer segment, a large proportion of brand loyalty is determined by the brand's match with Generation Y's individual sense of identity and what picture they wish to expose to others. Wood (2004), deems that attaining congruency between themselves and a brand will influence purchase and subsequently their brand loyalty in Generation Y consumers.

Marketers utilise strategies like loyalty schemes and programs to enhance the possibility of recurring purchase, and to gain critical data around consumers and their expenditure as suggested by Liu (2007). It has been documented that Marriot, Best Western, Intercontinental Hotels Groups and Hilton Hotels Worldwide have in excess of ten million loyalty program members between them Dekay, et al., (2009). Even in the face of the increase in loyalty programs witnessed during the last thirty years, it is been argued and questioned as to their success and profitability (Berman, 2006). Despite the large set up cost Wansink (2003), states that loyalty programs in marketplaces commonly fall short in understanding customer expectations and behaviours. Given the loyalty habits of Generation Y consumers, the continued use of loyalty schemes may not be the most appropriate strategy. It must be queried if consumers are loyal to the loyalty scheme/program or to the brand itself.

The Generation Y cohort are the first generation to be born in a digital era and are therefore highly connected. According to Google (2013), 95% of the Generation Y cohort used online platforms to complete their holiday shopping. As a result of these technological advancements, Generation Y consumers are discussing their purchase decisions and recommending the products they align themselves with to others both in person and online. Carter (2014), describes how this consumer group has the largest online research and purchasing rate of all generational cohorts, with consumers making choices on peer reviewed information. Smith, et al., (2007), suggested that in an information intensive situation, consumers actively manage supposed risk through seeking the opinion and approval of other customers. The resultant growth in third party platforms and online review sites ensures the information regarding hotel products and service delivery are no longer filtered.

Current Study Findings

In order to gain evidence for this study a total of five interviews were conducted with key hospitality industry experts, to assist in understanding the suppliers view of the phenomenon of Generation Y hotel brand loyalty. Two experts interviewed were from global corporate hotel organisations, with another two interviewees representing independent hotel groups. The fifth participant was an expert professional providing support services to the hospitality industry. In obtaining an understanding of the 'demand' element of the developing scenario, two focus groups, each consisting of between five to seven members from the Generation Y cohort, were interviewed.

Evidence from the industry interviews revealed that all four hotel groups investigated had a customer loyalty program in place. These programs varied in nature, with noticeable discrepancies between the loyalty programs employed by the corporate and independent hotel experts.

The two corporate hotel chains utilized a rewards style redemption program, where consumers earn incremental points based on the frequency of transactions and were able to redeem these points for future transactions, in the form of hotel stays and flights. This traditional style loyalty program did not prove popular with any of the respondents interviewed in either of the Gen Y focus groups. One independent hotel expert interviewed had a loyalty program where consumers earned points that gave them access to added value benefits, including Wi-Fi and room upgrades. It was apparent this 'added-value' structure for a loyalty program resonated with the Generation Ys' thought process in what they believed would make a successful loyalty scheme / program. The other hotel expert from another independent hotel chain did not utilise a loyalty point's scheme at all, but instead adopted a 'fan club' approach where customers who had previously experienced the product were in a position to gain added value through exclusive discounts on future hotel stay purchases. This rational of seeing customers as individuals with regards to a loyalty strategy also harmonised with the Generation Ys' viewpoint of loyalty programs that hotels should "Get to know me as an individual and give me something I actually want"

Just two of the Generation Y respondents were members of hotel loyalty programs and the reason cited for their registration to the scheme was for corporate travel only.

It must be noted that the majority of the Generation Y cohort interviewed, believed that loyalty programs and loyalty schemes would not be an influential factor in driving a purchase decision. This was due to the limited frequency of personal purchase transactions and that they felt that loyalty programs were not relevant to them as a consumer.

It must be noted that over 80% of this cohort had a loyalty or rewards card for retail products which were more frequent purchases with transactions occurring between the consumer and the brand on a daily or weekly basis. Examples of these were coffee shop cards, grocery shopping programs and restaurant and bar loyalty schemes. The frequency of larger purchases such as leisure stays in hotels were minimal by comparison, with the average number of occasions these Generation Y consumers stayed in hotels being four times annually. Due to the frequency of these transactions the large majority of those in the Generation Y focus groups cited price as the key decision maker when initially reviewing hotel options.

It was also evident that this consumer group was stimulated and attracted to purchase products that projected a representation of themselves. This was evident from a number of members of the focus groups who cited examples of brands outside of the hospitality context with which they emotionally aligned themselves to such as Virgin Airlines because they were considered cool and sexy. This view of Virgin Airlines, is an interesting representation on how some Generation Ys are connecting themselves with brands which they may potentially not be purchasing from but still deem to have an affinity to, solely due to the company's brand image.

This raises a thought-provoking theme of how this consumer group could have the potential to become 'brand advocates' in influencing other consumer purchasing behaviours, without necessarily having experienced or purchased the product. This further suggests stronger brand loyalty in comparison to program loyalty.

After analysing the qualitative research with regards to the Generation Y's views of customer loyalty, it was evident that their loyalty to a brand would be dependent on the delivery of product, service and personalised communication. However, discrepancies arise between the 'demand' and 'supply' chain elements when reviewing the concept of brand loyalty and loyalty programs. The majority of the hotel experts opinions were that brand loyalty is of an emotional construct, with the loyalty program being the vehicle that drives the rewards and associated recognition of repeat consumer patronage. Conversely, the Generation Y cohort regarded loyalty programs and brand loyalty as two separate entities that are able to be mutually exclusive. The perspective from the independent hotel experts regarding consumers potentially being loyal to the brand and not just the scheme, was shared with the Generation Y cohort where this notion was present in both focus groups.

The above responses from the Generation Y cohort clearly indicate that loyalty schemes in their current format are not deemed as beneficial or fit for purpose. They highlighted price, location and service experience as the key drivers in creating brand and customer loyalty.

When exploring the topic of brand alignment with the hotel experts, it was apparent that independent hotel chains such as Citizen M were clearly targeting this consumer group. In actual fact, one of the independent hotel chain experts elucidated how their company are actually targeting the behaviours of the Generation Y consumer, rather than the demographic age of the cohort itself. This was an important classification in that they viewed these behaviours as having a potential impact on the purchasing of other generational cohorts.

The industry experts unanimously agreed that this generation are less brand loyal than their generational predecessors. It was of interest to note that one industry expert explained that Generation Y may not be loyal to a brand, but rather loyal to the technology platform that affords them the opportunity to get the best available option.

It was evident that the industry's approach on how to gain this generation's future loyalty was fragmented. The two corporate hotel companies cited that the current schemes will remain in situ with minimal changes to the current status quo. This is probably reflective of the fact that change to these schemes on a global basis would be costly, and time consuming. The two independent hotel groups differed with one highlighting that personalisation would be extremely important in the creation of experiences. It was argued that this will become easier as sophisticated CRM tools are implemented across the industry. Early adopters will possibly leverage a competitive advantage from the resulting PR spin-off as a result of these individualised created experiences that are then shared virally through online communities. However the most interesting suggestion came from the one industry expert suggesting that it is too late, generation Y's loyalty is to platforms such as booking.com.

Peer to peer recommendation was also explored during the data collection with a view to understanding how important this phenomena is in driving a loyalty strategy with this generational cohort. It was overwhelmingly evident, that this was first and foremost the biggest driver of decision making amongst this consumer group. The hospitality industry experts acknowledged that the peer to peer platforms were particularly important for engagement with these customers. Respectively, each organisation had their own strategy implemented in order to monitor these online social media platforms. Nevertheless it must be noted that the majority of the hotel expert interviewees highlighted an issue of consistency of engagement across the various social platforms. Furthermore, there was a cause for concern regarding the vast amount of resources required to manage these channels effectively. Cost versus a direct return on investment was an apprehension for the hotel experts, however, all interviewees recognised that it was an important in raising brand awareness.

The Generation Y cohort had a preference for the channels they chose to publicly share their views and experiences. Interestingly, it become clear that whilst Generation Y used a number of different social platforms to gather peer to peer recommendation, the channels viewed were prioritised in terms of the degree in which the platforms influenced them. There was some scepticism around TripAdvisor's transparency with opinions that reviews could be potentially manipulated by hoteliers and their friends. Although public platforms, such as Facebook and Instagram were viewed as respectable sources of peer to peer recommendation, it was apparent that there was a rise in popularity in the 'closed and trusted' user groups of friends sharing recommendations and suggestions. It was evident that mobile applications such as Snap Chat and WhatsApp were actually utilised first when it came to sharing hotel experiences in the Generation Y cohort. This rise of closed user groups could become a potential threat to the industry as it invisibly influences the construct of peer to peer recommendation.

When exploring peer to peer recommendation and its influence on brand loyalty, a common theme emerged regarding aspirational emotions. It became clear that the success of the peer to peer recommendation could be defined by the level of aspirational emotions provoked. The more emotions the peer to peer recommendation obtained, the more likely the Generation Y consumer was to purchase or experience that brand – this was emphasised by both sides of the demand and supply chain. It became clear that this generation not only seek peer to peer endorsement for a brand or product, but additionally wanted to feel part of their peer's experience.

In conclusion, this chapter has explored the challenges for the hospitality industry in engaging the Generation Y cohort from a non-transactional basis with a view to driving organisational brand loyalty. It is of notable significance that this emerging consumer group are demanding a personalised and individualised experience in each interaction, particularly when engaging in infrequent purchasing transactions such as hotel stays. It will be imperative from an operational viewpoint to ensure an understanding of how this will be executed consistently, so as to enhance the merit of creating brand loyalty and advocacy. In addition, the preference for peer to peer recommendations and communicating by closed user groups could pose future challenges, for how the hotel industry will attract, drive, retain and commercially sustain Generation Y brand loyalty.

Reference section

Chapter 1

League of American Orchestras - http://www.americanorchestras.org/conducting-artistic-programs/conducting/traits-and-skills-of-a-music-director.html

Testa, M.R. and Sipe, L., 2012. Service-leadership competencies for hospitality and tourism management. *International journal of hospitality management*, 31(3), pp.648-658

Wack, P., 1985. Scenarios: The gentle art of re-perceiving, Harvard Business School. *Unpublished manuscript*.

Chapter 2

Garavan, T. N. O'Brien, F. & O'Hanlon, D. (2006) "Career advancement of hotel managers since graduation: a comparative study" *Personnel Review*, Vol. 35, No. 3, pp. 252-280

Harkison, T. Poulston, J. & Kim, J. H. G. (2011) "Hospitality graduates and managers: the big divide" *International Journal of Contemporary Hospitality Management*, Vol. 23, No. 3, pp. 377-392

Ladkin, A. (2000) "Vocational education and food and beverage experience: issues for career development" *International Journal of Contemporary Hospitality Management* Vol. 12, No. 4, pp. 226 – 233

Ladkin, A. (2002) "Career analysis: a case study of hotel general managers in Australia" *Tourism Management* Vol. 23, pp. 379-388

Mooney, S. & Ryan, I. (2009) "A woman's place in hotel management: upstairs or downstairs?" *Gender in Management: An International Journal*, Vol. 24, No. 3 pp. 195-210

Wadongo, B. Kambona, O. Odhuno, E. (2011) "Emerging critical generic managerial competencies, a challenge to hospitality educators in Kenya" *African Journal of Economic and Management Studies*, Vol. 2, No. 1, pp. 56-71

Watson, S. (2008) "Where are they now? A review of management development issues in the hospitality and tourism sector: Implications for talent management" *International Journal of Contemporary Hospitality Management*, Vol. 20, No. 7, pp. 758-780

Worsfold, P. (1989) "A personality profile of the hotel manager" *International Journal of Hospitality Management*, Vol. 8, No. 1 pp. 51-62

Chapter 3

Allen, M. P., Panian, S. K., & Lotz, R. E. (1979). Managerial succession and organizational performance: A recalcitrant problem revisited. *Administrative Science Quarterly*, 24(2), 167-180.

Dyck, B., Mauws, M., Starke, F. A., & Mischke, G. A. (2002). Passing the baton: The importance of sequence, timing technique and communication in executive succession. *Journal of Business Venturing*, 17, 143-162.

Fizel, J. L., & D'Itri, M. P. (1997). Managerial efficiency, managerial succession and organizational performance. *Managerial and Decision Economics*, 18(4), 295-308.

Guest, R. H. (1962). Managerial succession in complex organizations. *American Journal of Sociology*, 68(1), 47-56.

Hill, G. C. (2005). The effects of managerial succession on organizational performance. *Journal of Public Administration Research and Theory*, 15(4), 585-597.

Kesner, I. F., & Sebora, T. C. (1994). Executive succession: Past, present & future. *Journal of Management*, 20(2), 327-372.

Miller, D. (1993). Some organizational consequences CEO succession. *The Academy of Management Journal* 36(3), 644-659.

Chapter 4

Armour, S (2005), 'Generation Y: they've arrived at work with new attitude' *USA Today*, November 8

Barron, P., Maxwell, G., Broadbridge, A., & Ogden, S. (2007). Careers in hospitality management: Generation Y's experiences and perceptions. *Journal of Hospitality and Tourism Management*, 14(2), 119-128.

Buchanon, L (2010) 'Meet the Millennials' Inc Sept 2010 v32 (7): 166-180

Dries, N, Perpermans, R & De Kerpel, E (2008) 'Exploring four generations' beliefs about career: Is 'satisfied' the new 'successful'?' *Journal of Managerial Psychology*, 23, 907-928

Gilbert, J (2011). 'The Millennials: A New Generation of Employees, and New Set of Engagement Policies' *The Workplace* (September/ October 2011).

Haynes, P & Fryer G (2000). Human Resources, service quality and performance: A case study. *International Journal of Contemporary Hospitality Management*, 12(4), 240-248

Hershatter, A & Epstein M (2010). Millenials and the world of work: An organisation and management perspective. *Journal of business Psychology* 25, 211-223

Hewlett, SA, Sherbin L, Sumberg, K (2009). How Gen Y & Boomers will reshape your agenda' *Harvard Business Review*, 87, July-August 71-76

Johnson, J & Lopes, J (2008) 'The Intergenerational Workforce, Revisited' *Organizational Development Journal* 26 (1) p 31-36

Karatepe, O M & Kilie, H (2007). Relationships of supervisor support and conflicts in the work family interface and the selected job outcomes of frontline employees. *Tourism Management*, 28 (1), 238-252

Kerslake P. (2005). 'Words from the Ys', *New Zealand Management*, May, 44-46.

Knox, A, & Wood, J (2005) Organisational flexibility and HRM in the hotel industry: Evidence from Australia. *Human Resources and Management Journal*, 151), 57-75

Kowske, B J, Rash, R & Wiley J (2010) 'Millennials (lack of) attitude problem: An empirical examination of generational effects on work attitudes.' *Journal of Business and Psychology*, 25, 265-280

Millwood, A (2007) 'The young and the restless'. *Nation's Restaurant News*, 41 (5), 132-133

Myers, K & Sadaghiani, K (2010). 'Millennials in the workplace: A communication perspective on Millennials'organisational relationships and performance.' *Journal of Business Psychology*, 25, 225-238

Powell, S. & Wood, E. (1999), "Is recruitment the millennium time bomb for the industry worldwide?", *International Journal of Contemporary Hospitality Management*, Vol. 11, pp. 138-9.

Prensky, M (2001b) Do they really think differently? *On the Horizon*, 9 (6), 1-6

Solnet, D & Hood, A (2008) Generation Y as Hospitality Employees: Framing a research agenda. *Journal of Hospitality & Tourism Management* 15-4 59-68

Visit Scotland/George Street Research Ltd (2002). Stakeholder opinion research: baseline survey report, George Street Research Ltd Edinburgh.

Wood, R C (1997). Working in hotels and catering (2nd Ed). *London: International Thomson Business Press*

Chapter 5

Blakely, A. (2012). Top 10 Talent management Strategies for 2012. *On Balance*, 12-14.

Church, A. H., & Silzer, R. (2014). Going Behind the Corporate Curtain with a BluePrint for Leadership Potential: An Integrated Framework for Identifying High-Potential Talent. *People & Strategy*, 36 (4), 51-58.

Church, A. (2014). What do we know about developing leadership potential? - The Role of OD in strategic Talent management. *OD Practitioner*, 46 (3), 52-62.

Collings, D., & Mellahi, K. (2009). Strategic Talent management: A review and research agenda. *Human Resource Management Review*, 19, 304-313.

Kesler, G. (2002). Why the Leadership Bench Never Gets Deeper: Ten Insights About Executive Talent Development. *HR Plannung Society Journal*, 25 (1), 1-28.

McCauley, C., & Wakefield, M. (20064-7). Talent management in the 21st Century: Help Your Company Find Develop and Keep its Stongest Workers. *The Journal for Quality & Participation*.

McDonnell, A. (2011). Still Fighting the "War for Talent"? Bridging the Science Versus Practive Gap. *J Bus Psychol*, 26, 169-173.

Michaels, E., & Helen Handfieldones, B. A. (2001). *The War for Talent*. Harvard Business Press.

Srinivasan, M. (2011). An integral approach to Talent management.

Chapter 6
Ambler, T., Barrow, S. (1996) *The employer brand*, London Business School, London

Backhaus, K. and Tikoo, S. (2004) Conceptualizing and researching employer branding, *Career Development International*, Vol. 9 No. 5, pp. 501-517

(The) Conference Board (2001), Engaging Employees through Your Brand, The Conference Board, New York, NY.

Frook, J.E. (2001), "Burnish your brand from the inside", *B to B*, Vol. 86, pp. 1-2.

Hackes, B.L. and Hamouz, F.L. (1996), "Does training impact turnover and productivity of college and university foodservice employees?", Advances in Hospitality and Tourism Research: Proceedings of the Conference on Graduate Education and Graduate Students Research', Ed. K.S. (Kaye) Chon. Madisson : Omnipress, 1, 485-94.

Hurst, A. (1997), "Emerging trends in college and university foodservice", *Journal of College and University Foodservice*, 3.3, 17-32.

Main, B. (1998), "Big tippers can help increase DSR sales: Suggestive selling techniques for foodservice employees", *The Voice of Foodservice Distribution*,7.34, 65.

Sullivan, J., (2002), "Crafting a Lofty Employer Brand: A Costly Proposition,"ER Daily, November,25 (as cited in Backhaus, K.,and Tikoo, S.,(2004),"Conceptualising and Researching Employer Branding," *Career Development International*, 9. .(5), pp505-517).

Sullivan, J. (2004), "Eight elements of a successful employment brand", *ER Daily*, February 23.

Vallen, G.K. (1993), "Organizational climate and burnout", *The Cornell H.R.A. Quarterly*, 34.1, 54-59.

Chapter 7
Arnett, D B., Debra A. L., and McLane, C. (2002) "Using Job Satisfaction and Pride as Internal-marketing Tools." *Cornell Hotel and Restaurant Administration Quarterly*, April: 87-96.

Barron, P., Maxwell, G., Broadbridge, A. and Ogden, S. (2007) "Careers in Hospitality Management: Generation Y's Experiences and Perceptions." *Journal of Hospitality and Tourism Management*, August: 119-128.

Barrow, S., and Mosley, R. (2005) *The Employer Brand - Bringing the Best of Brand Management to People at Work*. Chicester, West Sussex: John Wiley & Sons, Ltd.

Chambers, E. G., Foulon, M., Handfield-Jones, H., Hankin,SMand Michaels E.G.(1998) "The War for Talent." *The McKinsey Quarterly*, Q3

Maxwell, R., and Knox, S. (2009) "Motivating employees to "live the brand": a comparative case study of employer brand attractiveness within the firm." *Journal of Marketing Management*, 893-907.

Miles, S.J., and Mangold, G.W. (2005) "Positioning Southwest Airlines through employee branding." *Business Horizons*, November - December: 535 - 545.

Shaw, S., and Fairhurst, D. (2008) "Engaging a new generation of graduates." *Emerald Education + Training*, 366-378.

Sigler, K. J. (1999) "Challenges of employee retention." *Management Research News* 22, no. 10 :1-5.

Solnet, D., and Hood, A. (2008) "Generation Y as Hospitality Employees: Framing a Research Agenda." *Journal of Hospitality and Tourism Management*, 59-68.

Terjesen, S., Vinnicombe, S. and Freeman,C.(2007) "Attracting Generation Y graduates - Organisational attributes, likelyhood to apply and sex differences." *Career Development International*, 504-522.

Chapter 8
Ehrenreich, B. (2001) Nickle and Dimed, Henry Holt and Company, New York

Leidner, R. (1993) *Fast Food, Fast Talk*. Berkeley: University of California Press.People 1st (2013) State of the Nation available at www.people1st.co.uk

Springboard UK (2012): "Young People's Perceptions to Hospitality as a career Choice and the factors affecting Career Choice"

Chapter 9
Baum, T., & Kokkranikal, J. (2005) "Human resource management in tourism", in L. Pender, & R. Sharpley (Eds.), *The management of tourism*, London: SAGE Publications Ltd., 1st edition, pp 86-102.

Beynon, H., Grimshaw, D., Rubbery, J., and Ward, K. (2002) *Managing Employment Change – The New Realities of Work*, Oxford, Oxford University Press.

Bratton, J. and Gold, J. (2003) *Human resources Management: Theory and Practise New York*, Palgrave Macmillian, 3rd edition.
Curtis, A. (2013) "The Brief History of Social Media" on www2.uncp.edu/home/acurtis/NewMedia/SocialMedia/SocialMediaHistory.html.
Fishman, C. (1998) "The War for Talent", *Fast Company*, Vol. 16, p 104 on www.fastcompany.com/online/16/mckinseyhtml.
IDS. (2013) "Using social media for recruitment, Income Data Services, available at https://ids.thomsonreuters.com/hr-in-practice/features-analysis/using-social- media-recruitment.
Jobvite (2014) on http://www.jobvite.com/wp-content/uploads/2014/10/Jobvite_SocialRecruiting_Survey2014.pdf.
Jones, C., Hecker, R. and Holland, P. (2002) "Recruitment and the internet: Possibilities and pitfalls, *IFSAM conference Australia*, pp 1-9.
Karl, K. and Peluchette, J. (2009) "Facebook follies: who suffers most?", in C. Romm Livermore & K. Setzekorn (Eds.), *Social Networking Communities and E-Dating Services: Concepts and Implications*, Hershey, IGI Global, pp 212-224.
Lawler III, E. (2008) *Talent: Making People your Competitive Advantage*, San Francisco, Jossey-Bass.
Lee, I. (2005) "The evolution of e-recruiting: A content analysis of Fortune 100 career web sites", *Journal of Electronic Commerce in Organizations*, Vol 3, Issue 3, 57- 68.
Lockwood, N.R. (2006) 'Talent management: Driver for organizational success', *HRMagazine*, Vol. 51, Issue 6: 2.
Mayfield, A. (2008) *What is social media*, (e-book), Icrossing, V1:4, updated 01-08- 08.
Singh, P. and Finn, D. (2003) "The effects of information technology on recruitment", *Journal of labour research*, Vol. 14, No. 3, pp 395-408.
Sison, V. (2009) "Social media -Attracting Talent in the Age of Web 2.0. Workspan", *The Magazine of Worldat Work*,
Stoller, J., (2012) "Recruiting with social media Online tools open doors", *CMA Magazine* (1926-4550), Vol. 86 Issue 1, p 40.
Tang Q., Gu B., and Whinston A. (2012) "Content Contribution in Social Media: The Case of YouTube," *Proceedings of the 45th Hawaii International Conference on System Sciences*, Maui, Hawaii.

Chapter 10
Bartlett, C.A. and Wozy, M. (2005) GE's Two-Decade Transformation: Jack Welch's Leadership, *Harvard Business Review*, May 2005
Florida, R., Goodnight, J. (2005) Managing for Creativity, *Harvard Business Review*, July- August 2005, pp.124-131
Ghazzawi, I.A., Martinelli-Lee, T., Palladini, M. (2014) Cirque du Soleil: An Innovative Culture of Entertainment, *Journal of the International Academy for Case Studies*, vol. 20, no. 5
Leavy, B. (2005) A Leader's Guide to Creating an Innovation Culture, *Strategy & Leadership*, vol. 33 no.: 4, pp.38 – 45

Chapter 11
Aaker, J. L. (1997). Dimensions of Brand Personality. *Journal of Market Research*, 347-356.
About Lifestyle Hotels. (2014, September 14th). Retrieved September 14th, 2014, from Lifestylehotels: http://www.lifestylehotels.net/en/ueber-LIFESTYLEHOTELS
Adner, R. (n.d.). *Lifestyles of the Rich and Almost Famous: the Boutique Hotel Phenomenin in the United States*. Retrieved September 15th, 2014, from Yumpu: https://www.yumpu.com/en/document/view/5320105/lifestyles-of-the-rich-and-almost-famous-the-boutique-hotel-
Day, D. J., Quadri, D., & Jones, D. D. (2012). *Boutique and Lifestyle Hotels: Emerging Definitions*. New York: BLLA.
Dictionary Reference. (2014, September 14 th). Retrieved September 14th, 2014, from Dictionary Reference: http://dictionary.reference.com/browse/boutique
Firat, A. F. (1991). The Consumer in Post Modernity. *Advances in Consumer Reserach Volume 18*, 70-76.
IHG aquires Kimpton Hotel. (2014, December 16). Retrieved February 15/02/2016, 2016, from IHG.com: http://www.ihgplc.com/index.asp?pageid=970#ref_kimpton
Mayerowitz, S. (2015, April 13th). *Travellers confused by growth of hotel brands*. Retrieved April 19th, 2015, from The Star.com Business: http://www.thestar.com/business/2015/04/13/travellers-confused-by-growth-of-hotel-brands.html
Wolff, C. (2008). Lodging's Lifestyle Landscape. *Lodging Hospitality*, 36.

Chapter 12

Beinhocker, E., Davis, I. and Mendonca, L. (2009) 'The 10 trends you have to watch', *Harvard Business Review*, 87(7/8), pp. 55–60.

Blanco, A. C., Oehmichen, A. and Frood, S. (2011) 'European hotel development – focus on budget hotels', *Journal of Retail & Leisure Property*, 9(5), pp. 373–379.

Bohlen, B., Carlotti, S. and Mihas, L. (2009) 'How the recession has changed US consumer behaviour', *McKinsey Quarterly*, 1(4), pp. 17-20.

Delgado-Ballister, E. and Munuera-Aleman, J. L. (2001) 'Brand trust in the concept of customer loyalty', *European Journal of Marketing*, 35(11/12), pp. 1238–1258.

Drakopoulos, S. A. (2008) 'The paradox of happiness: towards an alternative explanation', *Journal of Happiness Studies*, 9(2), pp. 303–315.

Ernst and Young (2013) *The hospitality sector in Europe*. Available at: http://www.ey.com/Publication/vwLUAssets/The_Hospitality_Sector_in_Europe/$FILE/EY_The_Hospitality_Sector_in_Europe.pdf (Accessed: 16 December 2015).

Flatters, P. and Wilmott, M. (2009) 'Understanding the post-recession consumer', *Harvard Business Review*, 87 (7/8), pp. 106–112.

Gerzema, J. and D'Antonio, M. (2010) *The power of the post-recession consumer*. Available at: http://www.strategy-business.com/article/00054?gko=340d6 (Accessed: 16 December 2015).

Gerzema, J. and Lebar, E. (2009) 'The Trouble with Brands', Strategy+Business, (56), pp. 49–57.

Hamm, S. (2008) 'The new age of frugality', *Business Week*, 42, pp. 55–58.

Piercy, N. F., Cravens, D. W. and Lane, N. (2010) 'Marketing out of the recession: recover is coming but things will never be the same again', *The Marketing Review*, 10(1), pp. 3–23.

Quelch, J. A. and Jocz, K. E. (2009) 'How to market in a downturn', *Harvard Business Review*, 87(4), pp. 1–12.

Voinea, L. and Filip, A. (2011) 'Analysing the main changes in new consumer buying behaviour during economic crisis', *International Journal of Economic Practices and Theories*, 1(1), pp. 14-19.

Whitebridge Hospitality Ltd (2015) 'EMEA Hotels Monitor', (16).

Yeoman, I. (2011) 'The changing behaviours of luxury consumption', *Journal of Revenue and Pricing Management*, 10(1), pp. 47–50.

Chapter 13

Belleau, B. D., Summers, T. A., Xu, Y. and Pinel, R. (2007) 'Theory of Reasoned Action: Purchase Intention of Young Consumers', *Clothing and Textiles Research Journal*, 25(3), pp. 244–257.

Hershatter, A. and Epstein, M. (2010) 'Millennials and the World of Work: An Organization and Management Perspective', *Journal of Business and Psychology*, 25(2), pp. 211–223.

Kueh, K. and Ho Voon, B. (2007) 'Culture and service quality expectations', *Managing Service Quality: An International Journal*, 17(6), pp. 656–680.

Sladek, S., (2013) Getting Gen Y to Buy. XYZ University

Tulgan, B. and Martin, C.A., (2001). Managing generation Y: Global citizens born in the late seventies and early eighties. *Human Resource Development*.

Wey Smola, K. and Sutton, C.D., (2002). Generational differences: Revisiting generational work values for the new millennium. *Journal of organizational behavior*, 23(4), pp.363-382.

Wright, E (2013) 'The Multibranded Hotel: New Efficiencies Through Innovation', *HVS Global Hospitality Report*, pp. 1-3

Chapter 14

Blanchard, O., 2011. *Social media ROI: Managing and measuring social media efforts in your organization*. Pearson Education.

Etlinger, S., Owyang, J. and Jones, A., 2012. The Social Media ROI Cookbook. *Six Ingredients Top Brands Use to Measure the Revenue Impact of Social Media, San Mateo*. Facebook (2013) Newsroom. Retrieved from: http//newsroom.fb.com

Fisher, T., 2009. ROI in social media: A look at the arguments. *Journal of Database Marketing & Customer Strategy Management*, 16(3), pp.189-195.

Hoffman, D.L. and Fodor, M., 2010. Can you measure the ROI of your social media marketing? *MIT Sloan Management Review*, 52(1), p.41.
Kelly, N., 2013. How to measure social media. *Indianapolis: Que*.
Macarthy, A., 2014. 500 Social Media Marketing *Tips: Essential Advice, Hints and Strategy for Business: Facebook, Twitter, Pinterest, Google+, YouTube, Instagram, LinkedIn, and More!* CreateSpace.
Powell, G., Groves, S. and Dimos, J., 2011. *ROI of Social Media: How to improve the return on your social marketing investment*. John Wiley & Sons.
Stelzner, M.A., 2013. Social Media Marketing Industry Report: How Marketers Are Using Social Media to Grow Their Businesses, [online] Social Media Examiner http://www.socialmediaexaminer.com. *SocialMediaMarketingIndustryReport2013.pdf*
Wendlandt, L.B., 2012. *Return on investment concerns in social media marketing: An examination of recent cases* (Doctoral dissertation, THE COLLEGE OF ST. SCHOLASTICA).

Chapter 15
Buhalis, D. & Law, R., 2008. Progress in information technology and tourism management: 20 years on and 10 years after the Internet - The state of eTourism research. *Tourism Management*, 29(4), pp.609–623.
Comscore, 2013. Marketing to the Multi-Platform Majority. *Comscore*, (October).
Green, C.E., 2013. My RevPAR is Rising But My GOP Is Not: Taking a Channel Diagnostics Audit.Magazine. Available at: http://www.hospitalityupgrade.com/_magazine/MagazineArticles/My-RevPAR- is-Rising-But-My-GOP-Is-Not.asp
Green, C.E. & Lomanno, M. V, 2012. Distribution Channel Analysis: a Guide for Hotels. A*N AH & LA and STR Special Report*.
Kracht, J. & Wang, Y., 2010. Examining the tourism distribution channel: evolution and transformation. *International Journal of Contemporary Hospitality Management*, 22(5), pp.736–757. Available at: http://www.emeraldinsight.com/10.1108/09596111011053837 [Accessed July 20, 2014].
Phocuswright, 2015. The Mobile Effect: Disrupting the Competitive Landscape in the Digital Travel Market. *Phocuswright White Paper*, (May), pp.1-11.
Runfola, A., Rosati, M. & Guercini, S., 2012. New business models in online hotel distribution: emerging private sales versus leading IDS. *Service Business*, 7(2), pp.183–205.
Schaal, D., 2014. Priceline and Expedia Are Google's Two Most Important Advertisers – Skift. Skift. Available at: http://skift.com/2014/05/21/priceline- and-expedia-are-googles-two-most-important-advertisers
Starkov, M., 2011. Special Report: Distribution. *Hotelsmag*, (April), pp.25–28.
Taylor, C., 2012. Expedia Buys Majority Stake In European Hotel Search Site Trivago For $632 Million. Techcrunch.com.
YStats.com, 2012. yStats.com - Research on International Markets. *Global Online Travel Report*. Available at: http://ystats.com/en/reports/preview.php?reportId=927

Chapter 16
Dellarocas, C. (2003). The digitization of word of mouth: Promise and challenges of online feedback mechanisms. *Management science*, 49(10), 1407-1424.
Dorsch M J, Grove S J and Darden W R (2000) Consumer intentions to use a service category *Journal of Services Marketing* Vol. 14 No. 2 p92-117
Kasavana, M. L., Nusair, K., & Teodosic, K. (2010). Online social networking: redefining the human web. *Journal of Hospitality and Tourism Technology*, 1(1), 68-82.
Litvin S W, Goldsmith R E, and Pan B (2008) Electronic word of mouth in hospitality and tourism management. *Tourism Management* 29 (2008) p458-468
Looker, A, Rockland, D & Taylor-Ketchum (2007) Media myths and realities: A study of 2006 media usage in America. *Tactics*, June, pp 10, 21–22.
O'Connor P (2008) User-generated content and travel: A case study on Tripadvisor.com Institute de Management Hotelier International Essec Business School p47-58
Schipul, E. (2006). The Web's next generation: Web 2.0. *Public Relations Tactics*, 13(3), 23.

Smith, D, Menon, S and Sivakumar, K (2007) Online peer and editorial recommendations, trust and choice in virtual markets. *Journal of Interactive Marketing*, 19(3) pp 15–37

Vermeulen, I. E., & Seegers, D. (2009). Tried and tested: The impact of online hotel reviews on consumer consideration. *Tourism Management*, 30(1), 123-127.

Chapter 17

Berry, L.L. (2000) "Cultivating service brand equity", *Journal of the Academy of Marketing Science*, Vol.28 No.1 pp128-37

Boone, M. (2000). The importance of internal branding. *Sales and Marketing Management*, 9, 36-8.

Brown, G., Chalip, L., Jago, L., & Mules, T. (2004). Developing brand Australia: Examining the role of events. In N. Morgan, A. Pritchard, & R. Pride (Eds.), *Destination branding: Creating the unique destination proposition* (2nd ed., pp. 279-305). Oxford,

Chalip, L., Green, B. C., & Hill, B. (2003). "Effects of sport event media on destination image and intention to visit." *Journal of Sport Management*, 17, 214-234.

Coates D and Matheson V. (2009) "Mega-events and housing costs: raising the rent while raising the roof?" *Working paper series*, Paper no 09-02, International Association of Sports Economists, February, Limoges, France.

Donaldson, R. and Ferreira, S. (2007), "Crime, perceptions and touristic decision making: some empirical evidence and prospects for the 2010 World Cup", *Politikon*, Vol. 34, pp. 353-71.

Doyle P. (2002) "Marketing Management and Strategy" 3rd ed, Harlow, Pearson Education.

Hamel, G., & Valikangas, L. (2003). "The quest for resilience." *Harvard business review*, 81(9), 52-65.

Hede A., (2005) "Sports-events, tourism and destination marketing strategies: an Australian case study of Athens 2004 and its media telecast" *Journal of Sports Tourism* 10(30), pp 187-200

Herstein, R., & Berger, R. (2013). "Hosting the olympics: A city's make-or-break impression." *The Journal of Business Strategy*, 34(5), 54-59

Jago L., Chalip L., Brown G., Mules T. and Ali S (2003) "Building events into destination branding: Insights from experts" Event Management, Vol 8 pp 3-14

Jago L, Dwyer L., Lipman G, van Lill D, Vorster S., (2010) "Optimising the potential of mega-events: an overview", *International Journal of Event and Festival Management*, Vol. 1 Iss: 3, pp. 220 - 237

Keller, K. L. (2002). "Branding and brand equity." *Handbook of marketing*, 151-178.

Kotler, P. (2000) "Marketing Management, the Millenium Edition" Upper Saddle River, NJ, Prentice Hall.

Moreland, J. 2004. "Olympics and television". Available via www.museum.tv/archives/etv/O/htmlO/olympicsand/olympicsand.htm [accessed 25 September 2013]

Murphy, J. (1998). "What is branding? Brands: The new wealth creators", 1-11. *Tourism Economics*, Vol. 2 No. 2, pp. 107-17.

Nadvi, L. (2008), "The ugly side of the beautiful game: the socioeconomic impact of the 2010 FIFA world cup on the city of eThekwini and its 'poors'", *World Journal of Managing Events*, Vol. 2 No. 1, pp. 39-47.

Punjaisri K., Evanschitzky H. and Wilson A. (2009) "Internal Branding: an enabler of employees' brand-supporting behaviours" *Journal of Service Management*, Vol 20, No 2 pp 209-226

Swart, K. and Bob, U. (2007), "The eluding link: toward developing a national sport tourism strategy in South Africa beyond 2010", *Politikon*, Vol. 34, pp. 373-91

Xing X. and Chalip B, (2006) "Effect of hosting a sport event on destination brand: A test of co-branding and match up models", *Sport Management Review*, 9, pp49-78

Chapter 18

Carroll, B. & Siguaw, J., 2003. Evolution in Electronic Distribution: Effects on Hotels and Intermediaries. *The Cornell Hotel and Restaurant Administration Quarterly*, 44(4), pp. 38-50.

Granados, N. F., Kauffman, R. J. & King, B., 2008. The Emerging Role of Vertical Search Engines in Travel Distribution: A Newly-Vulnerable Electronic Markets Perspective. Hawaii, s.n.

Green, C. E. & Lomanno, M. V., 2012. Distribution Channel Analysis: a Guide for Hotels. HSMAI Foundation.

Lee, H., Guillet, B. D. & Law, R., 2013. An Examination of the Relationship between Online Travel Agents and Hotels: A Case Study of Choice Hotels International and Expedia.com. *Cornell Hospitality Quarterly*, 54(1), pp. 95-107.

Ling, L., Guo, X. & Yang, C., 2014. Opening the online marketplace: An examination of hotel pricing and travel agency on-line distribution of rooms. *Tourism Management*, Volume 45, pp. 234-243.

Chapter 19

Auh, S. Bell, S. J, McLeod, C S and Shih, E. (2007) "Co-production and customer loyalty in financial services", *Journal of Retailing*, pp 359 – 370

Beatson, A. Coote, L. V. and Rudd, J. M. (2006) "Determining Consumer Satisfaction and Commitment Through Self-Service Technology and Personal Service Usage", *Journal of Marketing Management*, volume 22, pp 853-882.

Brown, C. G. Chun, M. and Koeppet, H. (2011) "Using Customer-Facing Technology to Create New Business Value: Insight From the Public and Private Sector into the Changing Value Equation", *Journal of Technology Management for Growing Economics*, volume 2, no. 2, October, pp 21-33.

Hsieh, Tien-An. Yen, Chang-Hua and Chi, Ko-Chien (2004) "Participative customers as partial employees and service provider woakload", *International Journal of Service Industry Management*, Vol 15, no. 2, pp 187-199.

Kim, J. Christodouilou, N. and Brewer, P. (2011) "Impact of individual differences and consumers' readiness on likelihood of using self-service technology at hospitality settings", *Journal of Hospitality & Tourism Research*, volume 36, no 1, pp 85 – 114.

Lema, J. D. (2009) "Preparing Hospitality Organisations for Self-Service Technology", *Journal of Human Resources in Hospitality & Tourism*, volume 8, pp 153-169.

Meuter, M. L. Ostrom, A. L. Roundtree, R.I. and Bitner, M.J. (2000) "Self-Service Technologies: Understanding Customer Satisfaction with Technology-Based Service Encounters", *Journal of Marketing*, volume 64, pp 50-64.

Meuter, M. L. Bitner, M.J. Ostrom, A.L. and Brown, S. W. (2005) "Choosing Among Alternative Service Delvery Modes: As Investigation of Customer Trial of Self Service Technologies", *Journal of Marketing*, volume 69, pp 61-83.

Peters, C. Bodkin, C. D. and Fitzgerald, S. (2012) "Toward an understanding of meaning creation via the collective co-production process", *Journal of Consumer Behaviour* pp 124-135

Ramirez, R. (1999) "Value Co-Production: Intellectual Origins and implications for practice and research", *Strategic Management Journal*, vol 20. pp 49-65

Reinders, M. J. Dabholkar, P. A. and Frambach, R. T. (2008) "Consequences of forcing consumers to use technology-base self service", *Journal of Service Research*, volume 11, 107-123.

Robertson, N. McQuilken, L. and Kandumpully, J. (2011) "Consumer Complaints and Recovery Through Guaranteeing Self-Service Technology", *Journal of Consumer Behaviour*, 11:21-30.

Chapter 20

Brown, J., and Reingen, P. H. (1987) 'Social Ties and Word-of-mouth Referral Behaviour', *Journal of Consumer Research*, Vol.14: pp 350-362.

Carson, P., Carson, D., Eden, W., and Roe., (1998) 'Does Empowerment Translate into Action? An Examination of Service Recovery Initiatives', *Journal of Quality Management*, Vol.3, No.1, pp 133-148

Chihyung, O., Ki-Joon, B., and Shanklin, C. (2006) 'Service Recovery Paradox: Implications from an Experimental Study in a Restaurant setting', *Journal of Hospitality and Leisure Marketing*, Vol. 14 No.3, pp 17-33.

Hart, C.W.L., Heskett, K.L and Sasser, W., (2000). 'The Profitable Art of Service Recovery, How the Best Companies Turn Complaining Companies into Loyal Ones'. *Harvard Business Review*, July - August 1990.

Hoffman, D., and Kelley, S., (2000) 'Perceived Justice Needs a Recovery Evaluation: A Contingency Approach', *European Journal of Marketing*, Vol. 34, No. 45, pp 418-429.

Kim, J., Moon.J, and Tikoo, S. (2004) 'Perception of Justice and Employee Willingness to Engage in Customer Orientated Behaviour', *Journal of Services Marketing*, Vol. 18, No. 4, pp267-272.

Krishna, A., Dangayach, G.S, Sharma S, 2014 'The Recovery Paradox: The Success Parameters', *Global Business review* 2014 Vol.15, pp 263.

Lovelock, C. and Wirtz, J. (2010) '*Services Marketing: People, Technology, Strategy*', Decisions marketing, No. 34,pp 100.

Magnini, Vincent, P., Ford, J.B., Markowski, E.P. and Honeycutt, E.D. (2007) 'The Service Recovery Paradox: Justifiable Theory or Smouldering Myth', *Journal of Service Marketing*, Vol.21, No.3, pp 213-225.

McCollough, M. and Bharadwaj, S.G., (1992) 'The Recovery Paradox: An Examination of Consumer Satisfaction in Relation to Disconfirmation, Service Quality and Attribution based Theories' *Marketing Theory and Applications*, Chicago: American Marketing Association.

McCollough, M.A.,Berry, L. and Yadav, M., (2000)'An Empirical Investigation of Customer Satisfaction After Service Fauliure', *Journal of Service Research*, . Vol. 3, No 2, p 121.

Palmer, A., Beggs, R., and Keown-McCullan, C. (2000). 'Equity and Repurchase Intention Following Service Failure', *Journal of Services Marketing*, 14(6), 513- 528.

Siu, N., Zhang, T., Yau, C, (2013) 'The Roles of Justice and Customer Satisfaction in Customer Retention: A Lesson from Service Recovery', *Journal of Business Ethics*, Vol.114, No.4, pp 676-686.

Spreitzer, G. M. (1996). 'Social Structural Characteristics of Psychological Empowerment', *Academy of Management Journal*, Vol.39, No.2, pp 483-504.

Tax, S., Brown, S., and Chandrashekaran, M. (1998) 'Customer Evaluation of Service Complaint Experiences: Implications for Relationship Marketing'. *Journal of Marketing*, Vol.62, pp 60-76.

Zemke, R., and Bell, C. (1990). 'Service Recovery: Doing it Right the Second Time. Management Review', Vol.27, No.6, pp 42-48.

Chapter 21

Berman, B., (2006). Developing an Effective customer loyalty program. *California Management Review*, 49(1), p. 123.

Bridge.Over, (2014). *Generation Y loyalty to hotel brands*. [Online] Available at: http://www.bridge-over.com/generation_y_loyalty

Bush, A. J., Martin, C. A. & Bush, V. D., (2004). Sports Celebrity Influence on the Behavioural Intentions of Generation Y. *Journal of Advertising Research*, 44(1), pp. 1-8-18.

Carter, L., (2014). *Millennial Branding: Creating Brands to Appeal to Teens and Young Adults*. [Online] Available at: http://www.personadesign.ie

Dekay, F., Toh, R. S. & Raven, P., (2009). Loyalty Programs. *Cornell Hospitality Quarterly*, 50(3), pp. 371-382.

Greenburg, K., (2011). *Study: Gens X, Y rely on research*, less on loyalty. [Online] Available at: http://www.mediapost.com

Houchman, K., (1992). *Customer Loyalty Programmes*. 1 ed. Nashville: McGraw- Hill, New York.

Markow, D., (2005). Childrens Reactions to Tragedy. *Young Consumers Insight and Ideas for Responsible Marketeers*, 6(2), pp. 8-10.

Noble, S. M., Haytko, D. L. & Philips, L., (2009). What Drives College-age Generation Y Consumers. *Journal of Business Research*, 62(6), pp. 617-628.

Richie, L., (1995). *Marketing to Generation X*. 1st ed. New York: Lexington Books.

Sebor, J., (2006). "Y me". *Customer Relationship Management*, 10(11), pp. 24-27.

Smith, D., Menon, S. & Sivakumar, K., (2007). Online peer and editorial recommendations, trust and choice in Virtual markets. *Journal of Interactive Marketing*, 19(3), pp. 15-37.

Wansink, B., (2003). Developing a cost-effective brand loyalty program. *Journal of Advertising Reasearch*, 43(3), pp. 409-428.

Wood, L. M., (2004). Dimensions of Brand Purchasing behaviours: consumer in the 18-24 age group. *Journal of Consumer Behaviour*, 4(1), pp. 9-24.